T5-DHA-907

Come Go With Me

C. Anne Davis

Woman's Missionary Union
Birmingham, Alabama

Woman's Missionary Union
P. O. Box 830010
Birmingham, AL 35283-0010
©1997 by Woman's Missionary Union

All rights reserved. First printing 1997
Printed in the United States of America

Dewey Decimal Classification: 248.4
Subject Headings: CHRISTIAN LIFE
                   MINISTRY

Scripture quotations indicated by NIV are from the Holy Bible,
New International Version. Copyright © 1973, 1978, 1984
International Bible Society. Used by permission of Zondervan
Bible Publishers.

Scripture quotations indicated by TEV are from the *Good
News Bible,* Today's English Version. New Testament: Copyright
© American Bible Society, 1966, 1971, 1976. Used by permission.

Scripture quotations indicated by NRSV are from the *New
Revised Standard Version of the Bible,* Copyright © 1989 by the
Division of Christian Education of the National Council of the
Churches of Christ in the USA. Used by permission. All rights
reserved.

ISBN: 1-56309-193-3

W973107•0497•15M1

Contents

Introduction/Foreword

I am deeply convinced that doing the work of missions and ministry is a matter of faith and call. The unifying, compelling reason for this book is that Woman's Missionary Union, at every level, believes that you and I have been called to missions and ministry in Jesus' name. It is our common prayer that faith in God will lead us to reach out in Jesus' name to the hurting people around us.

The aim of this book is to assist you in reaching out. In order to make the content user-friendly, it has been prepared in two major sections. The first section provides a review of the ministering model of Jesus. This biblical and theological base for ministry draws heavily on the Gospel of Luke. Its intent is to provide the reader with an understanding of why believers are to be out in the world doing ministry. It also provides a guide for believers to use as they prepare themselves for service in Jesus' name. The second part of the book is a "how to" manual which presents, step-by-step, the decisions and actions necessary to carry out an effective ministry.

In many ways, this book reflects my own pilgrimage. My call to ministry came in what used to be called a School of Missions, now referred to as a World Missions Conference. The place was Ebenezer Baptist Church in the Concord Association of Southside, Virginia.

The lives of that congregation's youth had been carefully tilled so that the seeds of missions and ministry could find fertile places to grow. We can give today's youth that same kind of preparation for receiving God's call. One of the most effective ways of doing this is to start a ministry which includes opportunities for youth to work alongside adults in ministry.

Throughout my 46 years as a believer, ministry has been the means through which I have expressed gratitude to God for my salvation. I am also deeply grateful to the people who have allowed me to be a helper in their lives. This book is, in large measure, a recounting of what God has taught me through these relationships.

Also, my gratitude to fellow Christians is enormous. One cannot do ministry without the supportive help of other Christians. I have found the encouragement, correction, and prayers of other believers to be both sustaining and indispensable.

My prayer for you, the reader, is that God will call you again and again . . . to challenge your church to see the needs beyond its walls, to prepare yourself by studying Christ's response to human need, and to follow Christ's example in witness and ministry.

1

Jesus' Model of Ministry

I t was the beginning of the Christmas season sometime in the late 1960s. School was over for the semester, and it was time for me to travel to Virginia to spend the holidays with my family. Arms loaded with suitcases and gifts, I trudged off to the train station in downtown Louisville. It was snowing as I boarded the *George Washington*, a safe and sure alternative to the potentially snow-packed highways of West Virginia and western Virginia.

By midafternoon, I had settled into my seat. Knowing I would not arrive in Richmond until early the next day, I pulled out a book to begin my self-entertainment routine. My reading was soon interrupted by a clear, commanding voice calling, "Tickets please!" Glancing up, I saw the train's conductor, his steps swaying with the motion of the train as he moved along punching tickets.

He appeared to have been doing his job for a long time. His snow-white hair contrasted with his black suit and conductor's cap, the bill of which was worn at the spot where thumb and forefinger had tipped it to hundreds of passengers. His coat pockets and cuffs were frayed. As I handed him my ticket, he tipped his cap and swayed on down the aisle, gold watch chain swinging. I returned to my book but kept an eye on the conductor as he moved back and forth through the cars.

Several hours later, I began to notice something curious. Whenever the conductor spotted a discarded newspaper, he stopped and picked it up. At first, I thought he was just cleaning up, but then I noticed that he was putting the sections and pages in proper order, straightening them, and rolling up the paper as if to ready it for home delivery. This accomplished, he stuffed the newspaper in one of his large coat pockets and moved on down the aisle. By the time we pulled out of the Mount Sterling depot, his frayed pockets were bulging with old newspapers.

At dusk the train started making its way through the foothills of Appalachia. We passed Olive Hill and headed toward Huntington and Charleston, West Virginia. By this time, my book was forgotten and I was devoting my full attention to watching the old conductor. After the lights of the Huntington station had faded into the distance, the train began to wind its way through the mountains. There was nothing to distract me from my mission except moonlight on trees, a few patches of light framed by windows, and the flashing red lights of an occasional crossing.

Somewhere along the line, I was startled by a blurred image flying by my window. I only caught a glimpse of it out of the corner of my eye. Since the old conductor had just passed by, traveling in the direction from which the object had come, I jumped up and followed.

I found him standing in the linking area between the cars, tossing yesterday's newspapers to people who lived along the right of way. Some waited by the tracks while others lived close enough to the rails for him to toss the papers onto their porches. All that night . . . until the last paper was gone . . . the old conductor connected with people as he "neighbored" them.

Here was a man who put together who he was with what he had available and transformed it into a ministry to others. He brought news to people who were tucked away from the mainstream. I doubt that he knew these people. However, he was there. The newspapers were there. The people were there. The need was there. The old conductor put it all together.

I don't know if the old conductor's motivation was based in a personal relationship with Jesus Christ, but his actions illustrate an important truth about witness and ministry. The resources, the people, and the need are present in our world. Jesus commands us to put them all together for the kingdom. Woman's Missionary Union encourages churches to take a fresh look at needs outside the church walls, then minister to persons with those needs. A study of Christ's responses to human needs should challenge us to follow His example in witness and ministry. A record of the ministering life of Jesus is found in the Gospel of Luke.

Nine factors stand out in this model of ministry. While these factors are interrelated and integrated in Luke's account, here each factor will be dealt with individually. The nine components are: (1) Jesus valued people more than religious traditions; (2) He included all people, especially the outcasts, in His ministry; (3) He identified perspectives that He expected His followers to have toward others; (4) He permeated his ministry with love and mercy; (5) He set standards for how other people should be treated; (6) He expressed specific attitudes to guide the use of wealth and possessions; (7) He outlined the cost of this kind of discipleship; (8) He called His followers to persistent prayer; and (9) He called all people to repentance and salvation.

1 Jesus valued people more than religious traditions

In *The Broadman Bible Commentary* on Luke, Malcolm Tolbert says there are two diametrically opposing ways to view religion. On one hand, religion can be approached as centering around rules and ritual regulations. In this instance, the main focus of adherents is to keep the rules and perform the rituals at the right time and place and with the right people. The other approach to religion puts people at the center, and Tolbert says Jesus demonstrates the latter approach.

Jesus' actions presented a problem for the rule-loving scribes and Pharisees. His behavior on the Sabbath was most difficult for them to accept. The rules and regulations for the observance of the Sabbath were of utmost importance to the scribes and Pharisees, but Jesus consistently broke these rules to help people. A few examples found in Luke are Jesus' healing the man with the withered hand (6:6–11), the woman who had not been able to stand straight for 18 years (13:10–17), and the man with dropsy (14:1–6). All these healings took place on the Sabbath. In the view of the scribes and the Pharisees, Jesus did things on the wrong day of the week!

In addition to these violations of the Sabbath, Jesus purposefully associated with people who, according to Jewish law, were outcasts. One example among many is found in Luke 15:1–2. Here the Pharisees and the scribes complained because Jesus welcomed tax collectors and sinners. To add insult to injury, Jesus ate with them. In the view of the scribes and Pharisees, Jesus did things with the wrong people!

Jesus enraged the religious leaders of the day when He refused to give them the sign they wanted at the synagogue in Nazareth (4:22–30). He went on to imply that Gentiles would receive benefits that would be denied the Jews. How could Gentiles be given things the Chosen People were denied?

In Luke 5:33–39, the scribes and Pharisees were concerned that Jesus' disciples were not following the same rules of fasting and prayer that the Pharisees' disciples were following. Jesus responded that His disciples would have plenty of time for that after He was taken away from them. To further clarify this point, Jesus told the parable of the problems one faces when patching old cloth with new or trying to put new wine in old wineskins. In the view of the scribes and Pharisees, Jesus did the wrong things!

The Old Testament rules and rituals existed for the purpose of guiding and helping God's people. Rules and guidelines were also established to help the young New Testament churches, but there has always been a danger in focusing too closely on the rules.

For the people who focused their religion on rules and rituals, Jesus created magnificent problems. In their view, He did the wrong things with the wrong people on the wrong days of the week. They would eventually have to get rid of Jesus because He was wreaking havoc with their traditional approach to religion.

2 Jesus included all people, especially the outcasts

Jesus made special effort to minister to people regardless of their economic, social, or religious standings. While He included all people in His ministry, He created a special place for those who were excluded by the religious and social communities of the day. Tax collectors and sinners, the poor, vulnerable groups such as women and children, people who were physically challenged, the demon-possessed, and even those who were sick with leprosy were helped, loved, and included by Jesus.

Tax collectors and sinners

Perhaps two of the best known encounters Jesus had with tax collectors and sinners are found in Luke 5:27–32 and 19:1–10. The first of these passages records Jesus calling Levi to follow Him. Levi then gave a great banquet for Jesus with many tax collectors and sinners present. The Pharisees and scribes complained to the disciples that Jews should not socialize with these outcasts. The second event took place the day Zacchaeus climbed the sycamore tree to see Jesus. Jesus told this tax collector and sinner to come down, for He was going to Zacchaeus's house to visit.

The forgiving of the sinful woman in Luke 7:36–48 produced the same reaction from a Pharisee. Jesus forgave the woman, and she demonstrated great love for Jesus. The Pharisee thought that if Jesus was a prophet, He should have known this woman was a sinner. The Pharisee thought Jesus should have stopped the woman from touching Him and gotten rid of her. Instead, Jesus used her expressions of love to teach Peter about forgiveness and love.

The scribes and Pharisees were responding naturally. The Jews were not required by the Law to help these outcasts if they got into trouble. Under the Law, a priest such as the one in the story of the good Samaritan (Luke 10:30–37) would first determine if the injured man were a Jew or a full proselyte, in which case the law required him to provide help. If the injured man were a member of the outcast group, the priest was not required to help. The law determined to whom Jews were to be neighbors.

Additional evidence of this aspect of Jesus' pattern of witness and ministry can be found in this story of the good Samaritan. The hero is a man who was considered by the religious leaders of the day to be an outcast.

People living in poverty

Inclusion of the poor is especially poignant. Jesus saw a widow put two small copper coins into the treasury (Luke 21:1-4). His heart was touched, and He said that she had given more out of her poverty than the others had out of their abundance. The emotions of inclusion ring clearly through the words of Jesus.

The same sentiments are echoed in the story of Lazarus and the rich man (16:19–31). This image of a poor man covered with sores who had nothing to eat and finally died is heartbreaking. But then he was carried away by the angels to be with Abraham.

Another example of Jesus reaching out to the poor is found in Luke 4:18–21. Jesus said that the Scripture in Isaiah had been fulfilled because He would bring good news to the poor. Zacchaeus, the tax collector, told Jesus he would give half of his wealth and possessions to the poor. At this point Jesus told the people gathered that salvation had come to Zacchaeus's house that very day (19:9).

In Luke 18:22, Jesus advised the rich ruler to sell all he had and distribute the money to the poor. When this was done, the rich ruler would have treasure in heaven and could follow Jesus. Jesus also encouraged people to invite the poor to banquets and luncheons (14:12–24). Jesus obviously had a special place in His heart for the poor.

People who were vulnerable

In the world in which Jesus ministered, children and women were vulnerable to social, religious, and economic exclusion. They were dependent on their families or husbands for basic necessities of life such as food, clothing, and shelter as well as social support. Children without families had no means of support. A woman with no husband was destitute. Yet Jesus included women and children as important members of the human community.

Jesus blessed the children in Luke 18:15–17. The disciples told the parents not to bring the little children to Jesus, but Jesus told the disciples to let the children come because the kingdom of God belongs to such as these. In Luke 9:46–48, Jesus had a little child stand next to Him as He told His quarreling, competitive disciples that whoever welcomed this child in Jesus' name also welcomed Him. He went on to tell them that the least among them would be the greatest. This was a new way for children to be treated and included.

At the time of Jesus' public ministry, women were considered little more than property. Jesus elevated them to a new status. He cured them of illnesses and visited in their homes. Many women traveled with Him and provided for Him and His disciples out of their resources (8:2–3; 23:27; 23:49).

The healing of the woman who had been hemorrhaging for 12 years in Luke 8:40–56 and the Sabbath healing of the woman who could not stand up straight in 13:10–17 are both examples of the tenderness with which Jesus approached women. He addressed the hemorrhaging woman as daughter and told her to go in peace. What a message to this woman who was so frightened that Luke said she was trembling when she found out she could not hide her identity! Can you even imagine what it must have been like for the other woman to stand up straight for the first time in 18 years?

The record of Jesus' visit to the home of Mary and Martha also illustrated how seriously He took the desire of women to listen to what He had to say. Mary moved out of the traditional role of hostess to learn from Jesus. He affirmed her daring action as being the better choice (10:38–42).

Luke liked to write in pairs, and often these pairs had a masculine and then a feminine perspective. In the parable of the yeast, which is preceded by the parable of the mustard seed, Jesus compared the kingdom of God to the yeast that women used (13:18–21).

Such a pair can also be found in Luke 15:3–10. This time the parable of the lost sheep is followed by the parable of the lost coin. In the latter parable Jesus said that the rejoicing over a sinner who repents is like a woman who has ten pieces of silver and loses one. She searches until she finds it and then there is great rejoicing.

What a difference this must have made to women when women they heard Jesus use their daily life experiences to teach about the kingdom of God! This was a new way for women to be treated and included in the community.

People with leprosy

The isolation of people with leprosy from the rest of the human community was a common practice in the time of Jesus. Lepers were required to announce themselves as they approached places where other people might be encountered to warn others of their presence. People feared catching leprosy and wanted no contact with these people who were considered unclean.

Jesus once met a man who was covered with leprosy. The man said he knew Jesus could make him clean if He chose to do so. He begged Jesus to cleanse him. Then Jesus did the unthinkable. He reached out and touched the man, and He chose to make him clean (5:12–14). Jesus did not have to touch him in order to heal him, but He did. Another account of Jesus healing people with leprosy is found in Luke 17:11–19.

People who were disabled

Jesus included people who were suffering from paralysis, blindness, and other physical limitations. Illustrations are found in Luke 5:17–26 and 18:35–43.

In Luke 5 a man, paralyzed and bedfast, was brought to Jesus by his friends. This is the familiar story of the men who removed a roof to lower their friend down into the room where Jesus was. Jesus healed the man and forgave his sins.

The Pharisees were disturbed by this forgiving of sin and questioned Jesus' authority to do it. The healed man went away glorifying God. In Luke 18 Jesus restored sight to a man who was blind and begging near Jericho. Jesus waited for the man to approach, then asked what he wanted Jesus to do for him. When the man replied that he wanted to see again, Jesus restored his sight.

Certainly these miracles served the purpose of demonstrating Jesus' identity, but this does not diminish the fact that they benefitted people who were considered unworthy of such beneficence by the religious leaders of the day.

Jesus included them all. Perhaps this review of how Jesus included the isolated, hurting, ignored, and needy is best summarized in Luke 4:18–19. "The spirit of the Lord is upon me, because He has anointed me to bring good news to the poor. He has sent me to proclaim release to the captives and recovery of sight to the blind, to let the oppressed go free, to proclaim the year of the Lord's favor" (NRSV).

3 Jesus required certain perspectives of His followers

Humility, not arrogance

Jesus made it very clear that His followers were to be humble. Christian humility always involves choice and power. It is choosing to take a lesser position when one could take a higher position. It is choosing lowliness over arrogance due to an awareness of one's relative position in light of the majesty of God. When the disciples were arguing over who was the greatest among them, Jesus said that the greatest would become like the youngest and the leaders would be those who served (Luke 22:24–27).

In Luke 6:37–42 Jesus made clear His intolerance of arrogance. This passage tells His followers that we are not to judge others. Jesus said our judgment is like the blind leading the blind. The picture of persons with beams in their own eyes trying to get specks out of their neighbors' eyes graphically illustrates the point He wanted to make.

This theme is further illustrated in Luke 18:9–14. Here Jesus affirmed a tax collector who begged God for mercy, rather than an arrogant Pharisee who thanked God that he was better than other people.

Jesus made humility a requirement of His followers. The attitude of the father in Luke 15:11–32 to the return of his prodigal son in Luke 15:11–32, the humble approach of the centurion who begged Jesus in 7:1–10 to heal his servant, and the seating arrangement parable found in 14:7–14 all illustrate Jesus' elevation of humility.

Integrity instead of hypocrisy

Jesus defined integrity as the opposite of hypocrisy. He blamed the Pharisees in Luke 11:39–41 for cleaning the outside of the cup while letting the inside of the cup remain full of greed and sin. He wanted His followers to see the need to let God redeem them through and through. In Luke 20:45–47, Jesus denounced the scribes who strolled in long robes just to be seen and prayed long prayers for the sake of appearances.

4 The ministry of Jesus was saturated with love

To say that Jesus was the epitome of love is a truism for those of us who believe in Him. The claim that the ministry of Jesus was saturated with love needs no defense. Luke demonstrates this with Jesus' conversation with the young lawyer who tried to test Him regarding eternal life (Luke 10:25–28). Jesus turned the question on the lawyer by asking him what the Law said. The lawyer's response, drawn from Deuteronomy 6:5 and Leviticus 19:18, was correct. The Law requires that we love God with all that is in us and that we love our neighbor as ourselves. Jesus told him to act out these commandments and he would live.

On another occasion, Jesus tried to teach Peter a lesson about the relationship of forgiveness to love (7:36–50). Jesus had healed a sinful woman, and out of her gratitude she demonstrated great love toward Jesus by bathing his feet with her tears. Jesus gave love and forgiveness to this woman who was a sinner and accepted love from her. Love is the foundation of the relationships that Jesus has with all who have faith in Him.

Ritualistic religious practices cannot replace the justice of God. In Luke 11:42–44, Jesus condemned the Pharisees for carrying out religious rituals and rules but neglecting the justice and love of God. This passage says that they should have been doing both, but the main point is that the keeping of religious rules cannot make up for failure to practice the justice and love of God in our relationships with other people.

The patterns of ministry and witness set by Jesus encompass more than just loving those who love you in return. In fact, Jesus said that to love only those who love us is of no credit to us, for even unbelievers do this (6:32–36). Then He demanded that we love our enemies and do good to all people, even those who hate us, and that we expect nothing in return for this love. We are to love God, our neighbors, ourselves, and our enemies if we are to follow the ministry and witness model of Jesus. If we include all of these in our love, no one is left out.

5 Jesus set standards about how we are to treat others

Jesus wanted to teach His followers that there is a relationship between how we treat other people and how we will be treated in return. The Golden Rule, found in Luke 6:31, is among the first verses of Scripture taught to children. Later in the chapter, other verses reiterate this message. Verses 37–38 admonish believers not to judge if we do not want to be judged and not to condemn if we do not want to be condemned. The verses also instruct us to forgive if we want to be forgiven and to give if we want to receive.

These admonitions are all simple, yet complex. They are echoed by the Luke 11:4 section of the Lord's Prayer, which states that we want God to forgive our sins as we forgive everyone indebted to us. This powerful section of the prayer makes it clear that the relationship between how we treat others and how we will be treated is not to be taken lightly by those who follow the example of Jesus.

6 Jesus specified proper attitudes for His followers to hold regarding wealth and possessions

Jesus specified several attitudes toward wealth and possessions that should be characteristic of His followers. He said generosity is required and greed is not acceptable. The love of God, not wealth and possessions, should control our lives. He also made it clear that the hearts of followers should determine what is important to us and how we behave. To let what we possess determine what we value and how we behave toward others is not the way of Jesus. Giving as opposed to hoarding was the approach Jesus directed Christians to embrace.

Believers cannot let themselves be controlled by wealth and possessions. Jesus told the rich ruler to sell what he had and give to the poor if he wanted treasures in heaven. This behavior was a prerequisite to following Jesus (Luke 18:18–30). He warned the crowd in Luke 12:15 to guard against all kinds of greed because life did not consist of the quantity of their possessions.

In the parable of the rich fool, Jesus described what would happen to those who kept trying to gain more wealth while being poor toward God (12:13–21). In Luke 16:13–14, He made it clear that people cannot serve God and wealth. In the parable of the sower, Jesus stated that seeds did not mature when they came to rest among the concerns, riches, and pleasures of this life (8:11–15).

Luke recorded Jesus' admonition to His disciples to sell their possessions and give alms (12:22–34). Jesus warned the rich that they had received their consolation here and that if they were full here, they would be hungry later (6:24–25).

These portions of Scripture clarify the attitudes that Jesus demands of His followers regarding wealth and possessions. They are not easy attitudes to establish and will bring people into conflict with current cultural expectations. However difficult this may seem, Jesus makes His claim on our wealth and possessions very clear by His words and His example.

7 Jesus outlined the cost of discipleship

The cost of discipleship is recorded in Luke 14:25–35. The brevity of these verses in no way measures the seriousness of the cost. Jesus said the cost of discipleship involves carrying the cross as we follow Him.

He warns us to count the cost before accepting the challenge. Because this will not be an easy road, some will not see it through to the end. Tolbert says, "Those who accept His [Jesus'] invitation must be willing to offer up all other relationships, interests, and ambitions on the altar of their commitment."

8 Jesus called His followers to persistent prayer

Luke recorded far more material on prayer than any of the other Gospel writers. An analysis of Luke's content on prayer seems to fall into three categories. The first category refers to prayer in worship. Zechariah's prayer for a son (Luke 1:8–13), Anna's enduring prayers (2:36–38), and Jesus' declaration that the temple is a house of prayer (19:45–48) are examples of prayer as a standard part of worship. Prayer is a vital element of worship.

The prayers of Jesus before, during and after the major events in His life form a second category. Luke records that Jesus prayed after His baptism (3:21–22), after He healed the man of leprosy (5:12–16), before appointing His disciples (6:12–16), before He announced His passion (9:18–22), before His transfiguration (9:28–36), before He taught His disciples to pray (11:1–4), before Peter's denial (22:31–34), on the Mount of Olives before the events leading up to His crucifixion (22:41–46), and before He died on the cross (23:46).

A third category of references to prayer focuses on the prayers of Jesus' followers. After teaching the disciples how to pray, He further directed them to be persistent in prayer (11:5–13). Again in 18:1–8, He told His followers to be persistent in prayer so they would not become discouraged.

In the verses following this admonition, Jesus told a parable about a Pharisee and a tax collector who both went to the temple to pray. The tax collector had the right attitude about prayer; the Pharisee did not (18:9–14).

In Luke 21:34–38, Jesus warned His disciples to be alert and to pray. Prayer would give the disciples strength to handle all the things that were going to happen before, during and after the Crucifixion. Jesus gave the disciples the last instructions about prayer from the Mount of Olives. In Luke 22:39–40, He told them to pray that they might not fall into temptation. Later, finding the disciples sleeping, He told them to wake up and pray!

One cannot read these passages on prayer without being awed by the importance Jesus placed on prayer both for Himself and His followers. Prayer was a vital part of the ministering life of Jesus.

9 Jesus' call to repentance and salvation

The Gospel of Luke closes with the appearance of Jesus to His disciples just before His ascension. Jesus opened the minds of the disciples to understand the Scriptures which had predicted that He would die and then rise three days later. He also told them that repentance and forgiveness of sins was to be proclaimed to all people. All of the ministering life of Jesus seemed to point in this direction. He left the disciples with the task of sharing the gospel and examples of how to go about doing this through both ministry and witness.

Summary
In His ministry, Jesus focused on people and their economic, social, and spiritual needs. He consistently placed greater value on people than on religious rituals, rules, and traditions. Those who were on the margin of the human community drew special attention from Jesus. His love and mercy were showered upon them.

His attitudes toward and standards of treatment for others established new ways of treating people. Those of us who believe in Him must conduct our ministries and lives accordingly. This discipleship has a cost, especially as it relates to our relationships, commitments, and possessions, and this cost is severe. We can endure only through much prayer to and mercy from God in Christ. Having repented and received salvation, we are told to share this good news with the world. This is the witness and ministry model of Jesus. Do this and you shall live!

Learning Activities

1. Write out the nine components of the ministering model of Jesus. Now read the Gospel of Luke. List the passages of Scripture you find that fit under each of the components.

2. Rewrite each of the nine components in your own words. Decide if you would add to or take away from the list compiled by the author. Think through each of the components. Commit your revised list to memory.

3. Rate yourself on each of these components by asking yourself the following questions: Which ones are problematic for me? Which ones represent areas in which I need to grow? Which ones call for changes in my attitudes and approaches to ministry and witness?

4. Are there groups of people in need with whom you can easily empathize? Identify these groups and think about why it is easy for you to understand their life situations. Write what you learn about yourself from this exercise.

5. Are there groups of people in need with whom you cannot easily empathize? Identify these groups and think about why it is not easy for you to understand their life situations. Write what you learn about yourself from this exercise.

6. Take note of any areas of your life or any of your attitudes that need to be changed in order to reflect the model of Jesus. Are you willing to risk working on these changes?

7. What is the role of prayer in your life? When do you pray and for whom do you pray? Are there items you need to add to your prayers as a result of reading this chapter?

2

Turning Stumbling Blocks into Stepping-Stones

Following Christ's pattern in witness and ministry does not come automatically. Jesus reminds us of this reality in the story of the good Samaritan. The priest and the Levite, two most probable witnesses and helpers, simply passed by an injured man. They did not get involved and they did not help. The problem was not that they did not love God. In *The Anchor Bible*, Joseph Fitzmyer says that their status demonstrated that they loved God, but it did not automatically mean they would respond to people in need. Witness and ministry are not automatic activities. They require study, prayer, and preparation. We must be intentional in asking God to use us as instruments to bring in the kingdom.

The challenge for us as Christians is to work continually to minister and witness as Christ did. This means that we must always be open to change and growth in our understanding of the example of Jesus as described in the first chapter. To accept this challenge is an adventure!

The truth is that many of our life experiences and cultural influences tend to shape our perspectives and beliefs in ways contrary to the those of Jesus. These perspectives and beliefs become hindrances as we try to witness and minister. While there are many such stumbling blocks, some seem to be more problematic for Christians than others. In this chapter we will identify some of these stumbling blocks, then examine guidelines Jesus gave us for turning them into stepping-stones.

Learning only through life experiences

One stumbling block to our witness and ministry is that we tend to trust our life experiences too much. Learning from what we experience is essential to living. Such lessons prepare us to avoid dangers and develop competencies that we need to live productive lives. People who cannot learn from experience are limited in both survival and growth potentials.

Children are taught at a very early age not to touch something hot because it will burn them. If they do touch a pot that has been on the stove and is still hot, they learn quickly from experience not to touch it again if they want to avoid the pain.

However, such learning becomes a problem if we let experience become the only way we learn. We need to examine the learning that comes to us through our experiences. Otherwise, we begin to believe our experience accurately reflects truth not only for ourselves but for all others as well. We stop being skeptical and begin to accept our interpretation of our experience as the final truth.

For example, if we see one person on food stamps drive away in an expensive car, we might generalize to declare that all people on food stamps drive expensive cars. We may then move on to shape a conviction about all people on food stamps based on this one life experience. We know people on food stamps drive expensive cars because we saw one person do it. Like the child who was burned by the pot, we assume all pots on all stoves are dangerous.

As we grow older, we learn to discriminate between pots that are hot and those that are not. We learn to think through the possible contingencies to determine if the pot is hot or cool. We then pick it up, with or without protection for our hands, based on what the evidence indicates. Since young children are unable to make these subtle discriminations, it is best to teach them to respond to all pots on all stoves as if they are hot. This childlike behavior is good for children, but not for adults.

Some adults never learn to make these distinctions and get locked into the "all pots are hot" way of thinking. This way of thinking can be convenient when making the subtle distinctions becomes complex and requires serious study, honest skepticism, and goes against what we have been taught to believe. We resist changing what we believe. It is hard to act on faith in a God we cannot see when our experiences, which we can see, lead us in another direction.

As a teenager, I would come home from school, change into work clothes, and find my father to see what work I needed to do. Often the assignment was to help him chase our pigs and put them back in the pen. Day after day they dug their way out of the fence.

I began to wonder if there was not some way to prevent this persistent nuisance. One day I asked my father about it. He responded that it was just in the nature of pigs to root and that there was nothing we could do but chase them down and put them back. When I persisted, my father said that all the pigs he had ever seen rooted. He went on to tell me that all the pigs my grandfather and great-grandfather and uncles ever owned acted the same way. Three generations of evidence was enough to convince even me that it is in the nature of pigs to dig their way out of their pens.

One day as we were working in the fields, a young man drove up in a jeep. He introduced himself as the new assistant county agent. Now, my father did not trust the United States Department of Agriculture very much. To add to the mistrust, this fellow was too young for my father to be convinced that he knew much about farming.

Insult was added to injury when the young man asked my father if he could help him solve any problems we were having on the farm. A twinkle appeared in my father's eyes. I knew what was coming. My father, winking at me, said, "Why yes, there is one thing you could do for me. Stop my pigs from digging out of their pen."

Without a moment's hesitation, this recent graduate of Virginia Polytechnic Institute and State University said, "Oh, that's easy, Mr. Davis." He walked to his jeep, came back with a little bottle of pills, and told my father that if he would put the pills in the pigs' feed, they would stop digging. Telling us that he would be back in two weeks to check on his problem-solving initiative, the young man got into his jeep and drove away. My father and I had a good laugh, and I stored the pills where we could conveniently add them to the feed.

We were true to our promise and faithfully put the pills in the feed. Then we began to notice the strangest thing. Chasing pigs began to disappear from the afternoon chore list. When I would go to investigate, I would find the pigs in the pen, seemingly content as could be.

Now my father and I faced an existential crisis. What do you do when the experience of three generations is suddenly challenged? What do you do when the evidence no longer supports something of which you were so certain you would have staked your life on it?

We could not wait for the two weeks to pass so we could find out what was in the pills. When the young assistant county agent returned, my father and I were waiting with our question. He told us the pills contained minerals that the pigs needed to survive and grow. When the feed we gave them did not supply this need, the pigs had to get it the best way they could, so they dug in the ground in search of the minerals.

I learned something important that day! I learned that life experience, even three generations of life experience, can sometimes teach us something that is in error. I learned that what we thought was inborn into the very DNA of the pig was not. I learned that when living things do not have what they need to survive and grow, they will try to get what they need the best way they can.

The survival needs in all living things are just as strong as in the pigs. Since that experience I have always tried, no matter how strongly my experience supports a perception, to leave a crack in the door through which healthy skepticism and openness might squirm. You see, no matter how certain I am of something, if I use my experience as the only base of knowing, I can be wrong.

Jesus teaches us the same lesson in the story of the good Samaritan. The lawyer wanted to know what he needed to do to inherit eternal life. Regardless of what the lawyer's motives may have been, Jesus entered the conversation by asking this expert to recall what was written in the Law.

The lawyer's response, drawn from Deuteronomy 6:5 and Leviticus 19:18, was correct. The Law said that the greatest commandment was to love God with all that is in us; and, secondly, to love our neighbors as we love ourselves. Jesus told him to act out these two commandments and he would live. But the lawyer, who would not let the subject drop, asked Jesus, "Who is my neighbor?" In asking this question, the lawyer raised an issue that dominates the witness and ministry agenda of many people.

The story is about a man who is traveling from Jerusalem to Jericho. Along the way he is ambushed by robbers. They beat him, take his possessions, and leave him in the road half dead. A priest and a Levite come along and see the man. Neither of them stops to help. Then a Samaritan comes along and ministers to the injured man with both immediate and long-term care.

Jesus has now set the stage to address this "all pots are hot" stumbling block. Life experiences of the lawyer had taught him that Jews help Jews. Throughout his life and for generations before him, it had been taught that a Jew's neighbors were limited to Jews and full proselytes. Tax collectors and sinners were not included. Under the Law, the priest in the story would have had to determine the category into which the injured man fell before he could determine whether or not the Law required him to help this injured man. Was this injured man a Jew? Was he a full proselyte? Was he a tax collector? Was he a Gentile? Was he a sinner?

Think of how puzzled the lawyer must have been at this point in the story. We are not told anything about this injured man except his life situation. We are not told who he is or anything he has done. John Nolland says in *Word Biblical Commentary,* "Nothing about this man mattered except his immediate desperate life situation."

Jesus adds insult to injury by making the Samaritan the hero. In *The Anchor Bible,* Fitzmyer raised the question, "Would a Jew normally regard a Samaritan as a model of kindness, picture him traveling in Judea, or think that a Jewish innkeeper would trust him?" Of course he would not because that was not what his experience-based beliefs would lead him to conclude.

It must have been as hard for the lawyer to start thinking about Samaritans in a new way as it was for me and my father to think differently about our pigs. But thinking in a new way was just what Jesus was leading the lawyer to do. The truth is that unless we are willing to think in a new way or put old things together in a new way, we are not ready to witness and minister using the model of the ministering life of Jesus.

Being judgmental

Another prevalent stumbling block for Christian helpers is our tendency to make judgments about who is deserving and undeserving of our help. This is especially true in instances in which a person's sin seems to have contributed to the need. We fall into thinking that we should minister only to those who are in trouble through no fault of their own and those who will responsibly use what help we provide. Because of this, many

Christians find helping innocent children to be more appealing or urgent than helping someone addicted to illegal drugs. I find no evidence that Jesus would have made such a distinction.

Certainly there is no problem with holding responsible behavior in high esteem. We all hope that we and other people will act responsibly. The problem comes when those of us who claim salvation by grace begin to separate people into deserving or undeserving categories. How can we claim grace for ourselves and be judgmental toward others?

This judgment becomes a more severe stumbling block if we can determine that the people in need caused their own problem or that they do not responsibly use our help, because as Christians we sometimes feel we are excused from further helping.

The ministering life of Jesus spins us around again. We can use this kind of thinking to build a case that the injured traveler in the good Samaritan story, by his own irresponsible behavior, contributed to his desperate state. It was common knowledge that the road from Jerusalem to Jericho was unsafe to travel. In *A Kingdom of Surprises: Parables in Luke's Gospel*, Cecil Sherman noted that even the Romans had not been able to secure the road. Robbers routinely hid in the rocks along the road and ambushed travelers. In *The Gospel of Luke* commentary, William Barclay described the traveler as "foolhardy and reckless." He reminds us that people who traveled this road did so in caravans to share the safety found in numbers. Apparently judging this injured man's actions was a nonagenda item for Jesus.

As you recall, this stumbling block of judging is addressed more directly in Luke 6:37–42. Here Christians are forbidden to judge and told that our only hope for mercy is not to judge others; our only hope that we will not be condemned is not to condemn others; the only way we will be forgiven is to forgive others; and the only way we will receive is to give.

These items are difficult for people to accept unless they know what it means to have experienced salvation through grace. They must also have experienced in day-to-day living what it means to be unable to rescue themselves from the mess they have created. The truth here is that we cannot treat people one way and expect to be treated another way ourselves. If we want acceptance, mercy, forgiveness, and blessings, we must extend these things to others when we happen upon them at some desperate time in their lives, regardless of who caused the problem or who passed that way before without helping.

Jesus added to this passage with the piercing illustration of the splinter and the log. It really does not seem to matter whether the people who are in trouble caused the mess in which they find themselves. What does seem to matter is that we know our own messes are likely our own creations. The point here is the attitude of the helper.

In Luke 18:9–14, Jesus told a story to an audience who believed they were righteous and who hated other people. A Pharisee and a tax collector were in the temple praying. Jesus declared that the tax collector went home justified because of his self-awareness.

The Jesus model of ministry calls for us to help others deal with their splinters while knowing that we have logs in our own eyes. Tolbert states that we cannot assist others with their problems if we assume a position of moral superiority. We must go out to help having prayed as the tax collector prayed. We do want God to have mercy on us because we are sinners. What a beautiful attitude. Whether a helper approaches with arrogance or with what Henri Nouwen calls "the wounded healer" attitude really does make a difference.[1] The first is not like Jesus; the latter is.

Compassion fatigue

Compassion fatigue is another stumbling block for many Christians who want to follow the Jesus model of witness and ministry. Roberta Hestenes defines compassion fatigue as a growing "sense of numbness which comes from constant bombardment with the images and sounds of human tragedy or crisis."[2]

Television brings images of starving masses into our living rooms. Incidences of violence leap at us from the daily print media. No community is free from domestic violence in the forms of child, spouse, and elderly abuse. Poverty and lack of affordable housing and health care coverage are just a few examples of the chronic problems that seem to overwhelm us.

In the face of these global needs, the tendency is to withdraw. We resist involvement in ministries of the church because we feel so inadequate. What can we do that will make a difference? Our hearts break over the needs we see. We want to help.

We are caught between wanting to help and wanting it to all go away. We are tired. We suffer from compassion fatigue.

Another way of looking at compassion fatigue is to examine the role we assign to need in creating our motivation for helping. If Christians rely on the existence of a need as the chief source of their motivation for ministry, they are inviting compassion fatigue or burnout. Human need does not in and of itself have the power to motivate people to minister to others over an extended period.

On the surface it seems that the needs of other people should be enough stimulus to motivate us to minister. Many believe that if we could just educate the people who have resources about the needs in their societies, they would respond to the needs. There is some truth to this statement. When reports of tragedies are displayed on television or appear in the newspapers, a great host of people do donate their time and resources to help.

However, the tragedies that appear on television and in the newspapers are for the most part acute, isolated events. Even in these situations, people who come to help can only stay a short time. As the days drag on, people have to resume their own lives and responsibilities. For example, think of the massive response to the 1992 devastation in Florida left by Hurricane Andrew. The recovery and rebuilding is still not complete, but much of the help has now moved on. Evidence suggests that need often motivates us for a only short time.

The only thing that has the power to motivate Christians to keep on witnessing and ministering day in and day out is what William Hendricks calls "grateful obedience to a loving God."[3] Hendricks is right. This is how the stumbling block of compassion fatigue can become a stepping-stone. Sustaining motivation for Christian ministry to people in need emerges out of our gratitude and thanksgiving to God for what He has done for us through His Son, Jesus.

If our motivation is based on the generosity, compassion, and love that God has for us, then our mercy, compassion, and help for others does not end until God stops showing mercy, compassion, and help to us. Since God is never going to stop, neither can we. It is that simple. It is that complex. We can endure not because of the nature of the problem or the nature of people who have the problem but because of the nature of God.

Appropriate role of needs

Having argued that need is not the proper motivation for the involvement of Christians in ministry, the appropriate role of needs must be addressed. Needs give direction and purpose to our helping. The properly motivated witness and ministry acts of Christians must address real needs, whether acute or chronic.

In 1988, while carrying out a research project for Woman's Missionary Union (WMU), I asked 334 adult members of WMU throughout the United States to identify the variables that were most influential in their decisions to become involved in mission action. The model of the life of Christ was cited by 96.7 percent. A comparable percent cited the teachings of the Bible. The variable reported third in importance at 95.2 percent was their understanding of discipleship. These women have motivation that will sustain them over the long haul. I doubt seriously that they will be victims of compassion fatigue or burnout.

Needs and Resources

The last stumbling block to be discussed has to do with the relative distribution of needs and resources. Often Christians tend to see themselves as the holders of resources and others as those who have the needs. This view results in a paternalistic approach to helping in which those who "have" help those who "have not." While often not intended, this approach has an arrogance not present in the model of ministry demonstrated in the life of Jesus.

The feeding of the 5,000 demonstrates the difference in the way people view the distribution of needs and resources and the way Jesus viewed them (Luke 9:10–17). On this occasion, Jesus took His disciples and withdrew to Bethsaida. The crowds learned where He was and followed. Jesus welcomed them and taught them about the kingdom of God. In addition, Luke wrote that Jesus healed those who were sick.

As the day went on, the disciples asked Jesus to send the crowd away to get food and lodging since there were no places nearby for them to eat. Jesus told His disciples to feed them. It does not take much sensitivity to see what the disciples were up against. How were they going to feed 5,000 men, not counting the women and children? John recorded that Andrew told Jesus there was a lad in the crowd who had five barley loaves and two fish (John 6:8–9). The stage was set for Jesus to teach His disciples a mighty lesson.

The disciples were overwhelmed by the amount of resources that would be needed to feed this crowd. Their first response was natural. They saw themselves as having to provide all the resources. The disciples did not have enough money to buy food for this many people. In addition, one could see that the crowd had been irresponsible. They had run off after Jesus without preparing for their basic needs. Many of us can identify with these weary disciples. It makes good sense to join the disciples in trying to persuade Jesus to send the people home to take care of themselves.

Jesus starts by telling the disciples to bring Him the loaves and fish. As you know, with the blessing of Jesus, the crowd was fed and a great deal was left over. During this process, Jesus made some things clear. From the disciples' perspective, they were expected to have the resources to meet this need. Since they did not, the only other solution they saw was to send the people away to fend for themselves. Here the role of the disciples was defined by Jesus; they were to go out into the crowd that had the need with the express intent of identifying the resources of that crowd. Having identified the loaves and fish, the disciples were to position these resources so Jesus could bless and multiply them. Jesus did not expect the disciples to have all the resources to meet the need.

Jesus was trying to teach the disciples that needs and resources reside together. No one has only needs. No one has only resources. Jesus knew the God of creation had not made the world that way.

God made us so that everyone has needs and everyone has resources. Helping is always mutual. We all must bring our needs and resources to the table. The lad who had the loaves and fish was a part of the crowd that had the need. That is God's way. Jesus knew it. The Jesus model of ministry calls us to mutuality, not an over/under perspective. What a relief to approach ministry knowing we are not required to have all the resources. What an even greater relief to know we are not required to have all the need.

Summary
Christians have a tendency to stumble when it comes to letting Jesus change our minds and hearts. It is not easy. When our experiences teach us something, it is hard to believe we are in

error. We tend to confuse making judgments and being judgmental. We are susceptible to compassion fatigue. We sometimes think we are the only ones who have the resources to get a task accomplished. These are our stumbling blocks.

However, Jesus can help us turn these stumbling blocks into stepping-stones. His model of witness and ministry is our example. If we are willing to pray and seek Jesus' help to become more like Him, He has promised that He will help us.

Learning Activities

1. Recall the story of the pigs. Identify something you strongly believe about people in need because your life experience has taught you that it is true. What would it take to convince you that you might have drawn a faulty conclusion from your experience?

2. Review the material on being judgmental. Does it describe you? Ask several honest friends to help you answer this question. Discuss your answer with someone.

3. Do you suffer from compassion fatigue? Are you overwhelmed by the number and scope of needs in your community? Discuss with someone whether or not the material presented in this chapter will help you overcome this compassion fatigue. Will it help you avoid it in the future?

4. What human needs are there in your community? Start making a list of these needs as they come to you.

5. Make a list of the resources you have that could be used to meet some human needs around you. What are your gifts from God? Ask these same questions about your church.

6. Begin to pray that these resources and needs can be brought together in Jesus' name. What will your prayers be like? Who and what will you include?

7. What programs does your church have for reaching
   out to your community with a witness and ministry?
   Investigate how these programs are working. If you
   church has no such programs, try to find out why it
   does not. Make yourself aware of what is or is not being done.

Principles ³ of Helping

The responses of Christ to people in need as recorded in the Gospel of Luke provide guidelines for us to use as helpers. Explicit guidelines were presented in chapter 1 of this book. Two implicit guidelines that can be gathered from the ministry of Jesus when viewed as a whole will be added here. These are the characteristics of a redemptive relationship and prophetic and priestly approaches to helping. Beyond these guidelines, two selected helping principles garnered from professional helping literature will be covered. These two principles have been selected from among many for two reasons. They have stood the test of time for effectiveness, and they have special application to church ministries. They are guidelines for confidentiality and referrals.

Implicit Guidelines

Jesus Offered People a Special Kind of Relationship

At the very core of the Christian faith is relationship. I believe it is the one universal modality of ministry. The process of building relationships is one of the simplest, and yet most complex, of all human experiences. It is through relationships that both sin and salvation enter the realm of human possibility. In its most common denominator, sin is the spoiling of our relationships with God. This spoiling also radically affects our relationships with our fellow human beings and with ourselves.[4]

Relationship is also the way through which salvation and redemption come to an individual. A right relationship with God in Christ is essential for restoration through redemption to take place in the life of the believer. The restoration of this ultimate relationship through salvation opens the way for relationships to be established, restored, and refined among people.

27

If restoration of the right relationship with God is the way people are saved and redeemed, then it seems that those of us who are Christians should follow this same model in our helping ministries. In other words, I doubt that much helping can take place unless significant, caring relationships are built between people. These relationships are essential to the heavy emotional and social traffic that moves back and forth between people who need help and those who offer this help. Helping is really offering to others, as much as it is within our power to do so, the kind of relationship that Jesus offers to us.

This helping/redemptive relationship is not just a run-of-the-mill kind of relationship. In *Giving and Taking Help*, Alan Keith-Lucas says that such a relationship is "an active and willing choice"; is "mutual and not one-way"; is "not consistently pleasant or friendly because it deals with reality"; has " a single purpose which controls everything that happens within it"; takes place in "the here and now"; offers "something new"; and is "nonjudgmental."[5]

These characteristics are not usually present in most relationships, and Christians are rarely taught the how-tos of establishing and maintaining helping/redemptive relationships with others, even though Jesus modeled them for us. Most of us have learned how to relate through our culture, religious traditions, and family models. We build relationships following these models and then we try to inject Christian outcomes into them. It just does not work that way. Helping people necessitates that we follow Jesus' model in relating. When we build these kinds of relationships, Christian outcomes are the natural results.

An Active and Willing Choice

Jesus offers us freewill choices. We are given the privilege of making up our own minds in matters of faith. Not only does He give us this active choice, He makes sure we know He will always love us regardless of whether we accept Him or reject Him.

The essential ingredient in offering an active and willing choice through relationships is unconditional love. When we offer help, the person to whom we offer it must have the opportunity to accept or reject that help without fear that they will lose our love, care, respect, and resources. In other words, our willingness to help and care should not be based on their response to us but rather on our commitment to them because we have experienced God's gracious and compassionate unconditional love. Carl Rodgers, author of *Freedom to Learn*, describes this acceptance as "non-possessive caring."

People who need help often try to figure out what will please the helper. They fear they will be deprived of what they want and need unless they conform to the resource holder's expectations. Once they understand the responses expected of them if help is to be given, the risk often becomes too great. They withdraw from the process.

The key factor here is power. The person who has resources always has power over the person who needs resources. Such power differentials are real and must be dealt with before the helping process can proceed. The only thing I know that neutralizes this power differential between people is for the powerful person to offer unconditional love to the less powerful person. Paul said of Jesus, "Who, being in very nature God, did not consider equality with God something to be grasped, but made himself nothing, taking the very nature of a servant, being made in human likeness. And being found in appearance as a man, he humbled himself and became obedient to death—even death on a cross!" (Phil. 2:6-8 NIV).

I had a conversation several years ago with a young adult woman. She was at that time a professional juvenile court worker, but I knew her first as a member of a club in which I had been a leader. As we had lunch and talked, she brought me up to date on what had happened to the others who were in this and another club. She mentioned person after person who had made a meaningful life for themselves and their families.

As I sat there going through my memories of these people, she asked me if I knew what had made the difference in their lives. I waited. She went on to remind me of the times they, as youth, had misbehaved and caused trouble. I smiled recalling some not so pleasant, yet vivid memories! She then said, "No matter what we did to try to run you and the other adult leaders off, you all stayed and came back year after year. Finally, it dawned on us that you all loved us unconditionally. When we realized this, it turned our lives around. We were never the same again." She was right. I know from personal experience that since I realized God loves me unconditionally, my life has never been the same either.

Mutuality

The relationships that Jesus had with people were mutual, not
one-way. A clear illustration of such relationships can be
found in the conversation Jesus had with the woman at the
well (John 4). Jesus was tired from His travel and stopped at the
well to rest. While His disciples went into town to buy food, a
Samaritan woman came to the well to draw water.

The first exchange Jesus had with the woman was to ask her
to help Him. He was thirsty and had no way to draw water
from the well. She had the resources and capacity to meet a need
He had. He started the mutuality of the relationship at this
point. Think for a moment. Here is Jesus Who could perform
miracles. He could have commanded the water to come up out
of the well and it would have. After all, He commanded the sea
to be calm and it did so.

The only explanation that makes sense is that it was important to Jesus to let this woman know He had needs she
could meet before He told her about the greatest need she had,
which He could meet. The need to establish some kind of mutuality is obvious. Jesus wanted to establish a common bond
with her even though she was a Samaritan and a woman,
which meant He was not even supposed to talk with her.
Mutuality is the point.

A key to establishing a helping relationship with others is to
let them know that we are all human beings and, as such, we
share pains and joys common to us all. It is never "we" and
"they." It must always be "us."

Have you ever been helped by individuals who seemed
intent on making you feel weak while they were strong, bad
while they were good, or dumb while they were smart? Recall
how it felt. Remember saying to yourself that you would have
to be in desperate straits before you asked them for help again.

On the other hand, you were drawn to people who commu-
nicated to you that bad times come to us all. They assured you
that they had been in similar situations and that they identified
with your plight. Remember how different this felt from the
other experience with the "superior" person? Redemptive
helpers present themselves as people who know what it means
to hurt and to need help because they have been there. They
share our common human needs. This is why it was so important for Jesus to be human and not just divine. He had to be

someone who experienced our pains and joys. He had to be someone with whom we could identify and share mutual life experiences.

Reality Focused

Redemptive/helping relationships have a reality focus. In fact, it is the presence of mutuality that enables reality to be the focus of these relationships. Jesus was able to focus on the hard realities of life for the woman at the well while deepening the relationship because He had set a tone of mutuality.

He told her she was right in answering His question about her husband. He told her she was right in saying that she was not married and that the man with whom she was then living was not her husband. Can you imagine talking this straight to another person whom you have just met? Yet this is precisely what Jesus did because He was willing to talk to her about the realities of her painful life situation.

If you study this passage of Scripture, you will find that Jesus was descriptive and not evaluative in the way He spoke of her life. He simply told her the "what." He left it to her to decide the "why" based on the new information which came as a result of hearing someone else describe her life. He helped her to see her situation from a new perspective. Once this was done, He gave her additional information about true, living water.

When people are approached in this way, they are often able to make life-changing decisions based on new perspectives and new discoveries about themselves. David did, once he heard Nathan's scenario about the poor man and his lamb (2 Sam. 12:1–15). He was suddenly aware of the devastating consequences of his actions on Uriah's life.

This reality focus is difficult for many Christians for two reasons. One is that while we are rightly concerned about sinful behavior, we can let this concern lead us to a focus on the "why" rather than the "what." When we do this, we become evaluative rather than descriptive. This leads us to tell people what they have done wrong rather than enabling them to discover this for themselves. In the first instance, they will likely remove themselves from us. In the latter instance, we will draw them to us.

The second reason that focusing on reality is hard for us is that we tend, especially those of us who grew up in the southern or southeastern regions of the United States, to believe that one of the greatest sins is to hurt someone's feelings. In order not to do this, we create what I call a "theology of niceness," which says it is better not to say anything than to talk about something bad. No one should bring up a subject if the other person does not want to talk about it. Jesus' conversation with the woman at the well would have been unheard of, or at the least considered rude, in my home town. Yet Jesus talked openly with this woman about things in her life that were very private, and in so doing, He touched her innermost self. She knew that this man was different from anyone in her village. The Scripture leads us to believe that her life was challenged and changed. Jesus never wasted time with cultural expectations. He cut through to the heart of the matter. He did it with Peter. He did it with the Pharisees. He did it with the woman at the well. He did it with me.

Single Purpose

Keith-Lucas's description of the helping relationship claims that it must have a single purpose which guides everything that happens within and through the relationship. The guiding purpose of the helping ministry is to assist people who need help. Certainly we want people who do not know Jesus to learn about Him and accept Him as their Savior. However, this choice must be a free one. We should be open and honest with people about our witness from the beginning. It is wrong to offer people help and then tell them that in order to get the help they must attend church or Sunday School so many times a month. Helping should not be used to entice people to come to Jesus. Jesus did not do it this way.

Witnessing in the helping process will come as a natural part of the relationships that we establish with people. If they accept Jesus, this will be an event to celebrate. We must continue helping them even if they reject Him.

Ministry is one very effective way to carry out the Great Commission. If we follow the ministry model of Jesus, we will find that people will be willing to listen to our witness because the way we have helped them has gained us credibility. We are believable because they have experienced something new in life with us. The very way we live and the way we treat them are different from most of what they have experienced previously.

Jesus did it this way in His model of ministry in the Gospel of Luke. We can do no less.

The Here and Now

The redemptive/helping relationship takes place in the here and now. If we dwell on the past, guilt will overwhelm us. None of us is without things in our past that we would like to undo. The future for many is riddled with anxiety. If we spend too much time there, anxiety will overtake us. People who need help need it now. We will stall them if our relationships with them are based on who they were or who they might become. Helping deals with who we are today and what we can do about our life situation today. Now is a new beginning, a fresh start. Tomorrow will present enough problems of its own.

This mental attitude is difficult for those of us who are members of the middle class. We really do want to live in the future. We buy great amounts of insurance to protect ourselves against the risks of our tomorrows. We have difficulty enjoying and utilizing today's opportunities for growth and change because of what might happen as tomorrow crashes in on us.

This does not mean that we should have no concerns for the future, nor does it mean that we should have no regrets about yesterdays. It does mean that we cannot make progress today if we spend an inordinate amount of time and energy on the past or the future. People who come to us for help need help with today's issues. This is especially true in helping them focus their limited energies and resources.

Something New

Perhaps one of the most important characteristics of the helping/redemptive relationship is that it must offer something new. Most people who need help have tried everything they know to try. They need new information, new insights, new solutions, new competencies, new understandings, new skills, or a combination of several of these new items.

Jesus came to show believers a new way. While it is true that many wanted to hold on to the traditional ways, Jesus knew that the new way was the only way. He offered the woman at the well a new Living Water. He told the rich young ruler to deal with his wealth from a new perspective. He responded to the tax collectors and other outcast groups with a new acceptance.

Ministries must offer something new to people who need help. It may be a new way of being treated. It may be a new resource. It may be a new competency. Whatever it is, something new must be added to the mix before change can take place. The concept of the catalyst is appropriate here.

Some of the people you will meet through your witness and ministry efforts may already be Christians. It is important to remember that Christians do have problems and needs. Life seems to crash in on Christians and non-Christians without prejudice. The assumption underlying some evangelistic efforts seems to be that anyone who has a need must be "lost." This is simply not the case. For this reason, it does not make sense to say that the first thing a Christian needs to do is to witness.

A more effective and natural beginning is to get to know people while ministering to them and then let your witnessing, discipling, and congregationalizing match the situation and emerge from this relationship. This way of witnessing will certainly have more credibility with hurting people whose life experiences have often taught them that Christians are not necessarily trustworthy or at best have an interest only in their souls.

This natural/relational approach will also avoid the trap of having people say what they think you want to hear in order to shore up their chances of gaining access to the resources that you have and they and their families need. When people make decisions to accept Christ, we want them to understand what they are doing; we also want the decision to be a life-changing one.

Remember that an unconditional love relationship with people in dire straits will neutralize the power factor between you and them. The absence of power will let people who have needs know that they have a free and active choice without running the risk of not being helped. This concept in itself will be something new.

Nonjudgmental
Again, the factor of not helping from a position of moral superiority is mentioned. The redemptive/helping relationship must be nonjudgmental as was outlined in Jesus' model of witness and ministry.

Word and Event as One
Peoples' lives change when their values change. The most

effective way to change values is for people to hear words that describe a situation and to have a life experience that gives feelings to these words. The other way is for people to have an experience and then hear words which describe and interpret this experience. A key, of course, is that the word and event must take place in a relatively close time frame. For example, people who go on partnership missions trips often return saying that their lives have been changed. This change occurs because they have had a word and event experience. What they know in a cognitive sense and what they have felt in an affective sense are now one and the same. This internal consistency within people causes growth to take place.

However, what people think and what they feel can be opposites. If they are opposite, the dissonance makes these individuals extremely uncomfortable. Since people generally want to avoid discomfort, there are two possible ways to deal with this discomfort. Either we can split or separate our words and events and pretend that there is no connection, or we can change to make them consistent and thereby relieve our discomfort.

For example, Mrs. Smith has a certain prejudice against people on welfare. She has heard a lot of words spoken about people who "go on welfare" because they are lazy and do not want to work. She accepts these words as true. Recently Mrs. Smith's Women on Mission* group decided to volunteer at a local homeless shelter. In the course of this experience, Mrs. Smith met members of several young families living in the shelter. They shared their stories with her. Her heart was touched and she felt great sorrow for these people who had tried and tried to find work and could not. When she learned that they had to resort to welfare, Mrs. Smith became very uncomfortable. What she believed about these people and what she felt about these people were in opposition. To get rid of this discomfort, Mrs. Smith can block what she has experienced, withdraw from the homeless shelter, reinforce what she accepted to be true, and live happily ever after, or she can change her values by adjusting what she had accepted as being true. If Mrs. Smith chooses to split the two, word and event, her values will not change. If she chooses to adjust what she has accepted as being true, then she has changed her values. This change in her values will ultimately result in a change in her behavior.

Jesus is both word and event at the same time. When we accept Him, our values and lives are changed. This process of change that takes place in us when we become believers is the same process as described in Mrs. Smith's case. The uniqueness is that Jesus helps us to be willing to take the risk of changing. Jesus will help us work out the inconsistencies within ourselves.

Jesus' coming to earth to be with us was and is a major event in the life of all believers. He came in the flesh because God knew from experience that a covenant of words only would not work. Beginning with the children of Israel, a covenant of words was not something that could be kept. No matter how many promises they made, they always broke them. So God sent us an event of grace, and His name was Jesus. His presence with us allows us to pull together word and event as never before. Scripture tells us that the Word became flesh and dwelt among us. Now that we have the event and the Word, life can be changed.

Look first at people who hear words and are taught only through verbal communication. These people can develop a set of beliefs to which they have strong allegiances. They will be able to define and communicate these beliefs as principles. They vow that they use these principles to guide their interactions with other people. However, in reality they do not. Beliefs about social justice can be used to illustrate this point.

People will tell you they are strong believers in social justice. However, when they meet another person on the street, it never occurs to them to let this belief system guide their interactions. Instead they generally act out of a pool of feelings which have nothing to do with justice. In other words, we generally set aside our belief systems and act out of our feelings. In some instances we can set aside our feelings and act out of our beliefs. However, this is much more difficult to do because it requires intentional effort.

In fact, this pool of feelings may be filled with prejudices set in place by life experiences, role models, or cultural expectations passed on through many generations. Such prejudice is evidenced by the way many Christians discriminate against people of other races and ethnic origins. They can say that they understand what justice for all people means. They will testify that they do not want to hurt anyone. However, in their daily lives, they are unable or unwilling to cease discrimination.

Such people have split word and event, and event is the main forger of their actions even though they know better and believe better.

Real changes in people's lives come when words explain events and these events reinforce the meanings of the words. I know of no other way that it happens. Jesus never split these two. His words always interpreted His actions. His actions always reaffirmed His words. Human beings need this internal consistency if they are to experience lasting changes in their lives.

We must offer this kind of consistency and integrity in our relationships to others. What we do and what we say or promise must match. Hurting people have already suffered enough at the hands of people who believe one thing and do another. Because of this pain, they can sense when this is happening again. Unless we act as we say we believe and unless our beliefs affirm our actions, no amount of pretending on our part will work. They will know. People who come to us for help are looking for real people. Jesus offered this and so must we.

Prophetic and Priestly Helping

In Vacation Bible School I was taught that priests were those people who carried the message of the people to God and that prophets brought God's message to the people. From these two different roles there have emerged two different kinds of helping. I call them priestly and prophetic helping. Priestly helping involves working with individuals, families, and small groups to solve problems. It entails face-to-face encounters between the helper and those needing help. Prophetic helping involves social justice and social change directed at the larger, oppressing systems of society. Jesus modeled both priestly and prophetic helping.

Jesus helped people on an individual level. He healed the sick, clothed the naked, and fed the hungry. He related to people as individuals, and Luke records many of these instances of priestly helping. Jesus showed great tenderness, mercy, and compassion to persons as He went along His way. His model calls for us to do the same.

However, Jesus did not stop with the individual, the family, or the small group. Luke records many examples of Jesus taking on the religious power brokers and their laws and traditions. He confronted the structures that oppressed people. He was an agent of change at the systems levels. He made it plain that the good news was for everyone, not just those who were approved by the religious traditions of the Pharisees. He cleansed the temple and drove out the money changers. On numerous occasions He violated the Sabbath laws in favor of helping people. There are other examples of this kind of prophetic helping recorded in Luke.

In the Jesus model of ministry and witness, we have examples of Jesus helping both on an individual level and on a larger structural level. These approaches are further clarified in Micah 6:6–8, the famous passage concerning the nature of true religion. This Scripture relates that we are to do justice, love kindness, and walk humbly with our God. Page Kelly says that to do justice means "to set right what is wrong and protect the rights of the weak and defenseless members of society. When a nation's system of justice breaks down, or when it protects only the rich and allows them to exploit the poor with impunity, that nation is sowing the seeds of its own destruction." He goes on to say that to love kindness means "to love someone whose only claim on our love is his or her need to be loved." Further Kelly says that to walk humbly with our God means "to keep in step with God."[6]

We, too, are called to help on both levels. While it is essential that we help individuals, we must also take on the religious power brokers who foster oppressive exclusions of people from the household of faith. For example, in 1996 Woman's Missionary Union selected AIDS as its annual social issue ministry emphasis. On several occasions, women related to me that they had difficulty getting the leadership of their churches to support their year's ministries to people living with AIDS and their families. Apparently, these religious leaders became so concerned about what others might think of them for getting involved with people with AIDS that they could not bring themselves to enter the arena of helping these patients and their families. Jesus fought the established religious order of His day for similar behaviors related to people with leprosy. Jesus confronted this kind of action taken in the name of religious traditions.

Another example of individual and structural approaches to helping can be seen in ethnic and racial discrimination. Some progress has been made in overcoming our prejudice on an individual level. Our attitudes and approaches to people of different races and ethnic heritages have become much more inclusive, but in recent years we have faltered.

However, institutional racism has, for the most part, been left in place. We have yet to address the major discriminations that take place in our society at institutional and larger system levels. We get very uncomfortable when we are asked questions about why most people in prison are African American or why Latino babies have a much lower rate of survival than Anglo babies born in America. We have no answer when asked why women earn about 75 percent of what men earn who do the same job at the same level of satisfaction. These are structural issues that will never be changed as long as we limit our helping to working with an individual in a prison ministry, to teaching a Latino mother parenting skills, or to helping a woman buy groceries because she ran out of money.

It was precisely at this point of confronting religious traditions and religious power brokers that Jesus encountered the troubles that eventually took Him to the cross. Regardless of the consequences, He did it. And He calls us to help individuals and to work to bring about changes in the oppressing religious traditions and larger structures of our society.

Perhaps the best way to summarize this point is to put together the three aspects of true religion as Kelly described them in his commentary. True religion means to set right what is wrong and thereby do justice, to love people because they need our love and thereby love kindness, and to keep in step with God as we do these two thereby walking humbly with our God.

Guidelines from Helping Literature

Referrals

Referral is an enabling process by which persons with defined needs are made aware of and helped to utilize professional resources that are located within their community and are designed to meet these needs.[7] However, it is necessary to remember that every helper, professional or volunteer, cannot, and in some cases should not, try to help a particular person. One of the first principles of helping is to know your goals and limitations. Do what you know how to do, but never move beyond your competencies. If you do, people will not likely be helped. In fact, in some instances they may be hurt. Certainly you will experience frustration and discouragement when you get too far out on a limb trying to help. The key is to do what you know how to do as long as it is within the goals of the ministry you are representing. Good helpers are always ready to acknowledge their limitations.

When someone asks you for help, there are three questions you need to ask and answer before agreeing to become involved or before implicitly making any promises to help.

A. Do the goals of our ministry include meeting this identified need? Is this something we have decided to do?

The purpose of the goal of any ministry is to keep the ministry effort focused. You will become aware of many needs as you go along. If you try to meet them all, you will become over-extended and fragmented. In the end you will lose your intended focus and accomplish little. Stay on track with what you set out to do. If you decide that this defined need is within your ministry goals, go to the next question. If it is not, make a referral to another agency whose goal it is to meet this need.

B. Do I know how to help this person meet this need?

You will need to follow your own judgment in answering this question. If you think you know how to help, go on to the next question. If you do not think you know how to help this person, a referral is indicated.

C. Am I comfortable about this entire situation?

My experience tells me that most people are comfortable when things are right and uncomfortable when they are not. This seems to be true even when helpers have not been able to verbalize their discomfort. If something does not seem right, then it probably is not. If you answer in the affirmative, get involved. If your answer is negative, referral is indicated.

Yes answers to all three of these questions mean that you should go ahead and risk getting involved. If you answer no to any of the three, refer the person to someone else who can help them meet the particular need. You will not remove yourself from the process. Instead, you will play the role of supporter and encourager rather than primary helper.

Sometimes, even when you answer all three of these questions in the affirmative and get involved, you may find out later that a referral is needed. This usually happens when, in the course of helping, you learn that the presenting problem was not the real problem. This redefinition or reframing of the identified need may indicate a need to revisit the three questions all over again. For example, you have agreed to tutor an elementary school child in remedial reading. Lately the child has begun to fall behind in reading competency. In conversation with the child you learn that she is having trouble seeing the words on the page. You check with the school counselor and find that the child's parents cannot afford to purchase corrective lenses for her.

You are a member of a professional woman's club that buys glasses for children living below the poverty line. Through the guidance counselor, you refer the child and her parents to a local clinic with whom the professional woman's club is working. The child gets new glasses. You then pick up again with the tutoring sessions. All during this referral process you have encouraged the child and the guidance counselor as they worked with the family and the clinic.

Resources and Consultants

A word needs to be said here about resources and consultants before returning to our discussion of referrals. Part of helping requires that you have a knowledge of other helpers in your community to whom you can refer people or to whom you can go for consultation when you are stymied. For example, it is recommended practice that helpers have others in the helping network to whom they can turn for assistance.

Usually in larger cities the United Way or some other umbrella organization will publish a directory of social, physical health, mental health, and other helping organizations. I recommend that churches starting ministries secure a copy of this directory if one is available. If one is not available, a group of church members can compile such a directory by calling public service agencies, schools, churches, social service agencies, health and human service agencies, and any other agency that may be unique to your location.

If a group from your church assumes responsibility for compiling a directory of community resources, there are a number of pieces of information they will need to collect to ensure that successful referrals can be made. Basic information that needs to be gathered includes name of agency, mailing address, geographic location, phone number, fax number, fees for services offered, client eligibility requirements, names of contact persons, credentials of helping staff, and licensing status if applicable. In addition, the compiling group needs to find out if the person coming for help needs to bring any papers or documents to the initial interview. Birth certificates, medical records, immunization records, proof of employment, and social security or tax identification numbers are examples of some of the documents often required. It may be helpful to know if the initial contact can be made by phone or if the person is required to appear. After all this information is secured, it may be wise to ask the person providing information about this service an open ended question such as, Is there anything I missed that I would need to know to refer someone to your service?

In the matter of consultation, you may not need to refer someone to another service agency. Instead, you may need to consult with a member of the professional helping network to seek a piece of information or consult with a professional on a matter related to a particular helping situation.

Be sure to ask if there are members of your congregation or other congregations in your association who could serve as consultants in particular areas. Lawyers, social workers, psychiatrists, physicians, nurses, police officers, fire fighters, and disaster and emergency officers are a few examples of the kinds of people you need to have access to for consultations. Have a mental health professional who can consult with you on matters related to mental health and medications. Get to know someone at the nearest drug and alcohol detoxification or treatment program in the event that you need advice or information on matters of chemical dependency.

Most helping professionals will be generous with their time and expertise. If you want to discuss a particular client, helping professionals will not release information to you unless you have the permission of the client in writing. The same is true for you. Before you talk to a consultant, ask the client's permission to discuss the situation with the consultant. You can do this by telling the client that you think it will help if you can get a third opinion on the issue at hand since neither of you is an expert on the subject. Clients will usually give permission because they want all the help they can get. This request may take more time, but it safeguards confidentiality and the client's legal right to privacy.

Now returning to the discussion on referrals . . . they are generally made by carrying out the following steps. First, the reason for the referral should be explained to everyone involved. For example, in your ministry with the elderly, an older woman wants you to help her understand the side effects of several of the medications she is taking. When you examine all the bottles of medicine she shows you, you begin to wonder if she is taking too much medicine. Perhaps you recently read in the newspaper that two of her medicines should not be taken together. You notice that each of these medications has been prescribed by a different physician. Now there are several concerns. She wants to know about side effects; you are concerned with overmedication and drug interactions.

This situation brings up several issues which have to be addressed. First, if you are not a physician, you have to make plain to her that you cannot give advice or information about her medications. To do so would open a number of legal liability issues that you must avoid. However, with her permission you are willing to assist her in communicating with her personal physician to see that she gets the information she needs. You must make sure that her physician gets all the information she needs about her medications. With the client's permission, you can ask her physician about issues that concern you. You have begun the referral process.

The second step is to gather all the information you will need in order to make the referral. This means writing down each drug that she is taking, the amount and frequency of the dosages, the issue dates, the names of the doctors who prescribed each medication, and the pharmacies that filled the prescriptions. Make sure, as best you can, that you have all of this information.

Then assist the woman in making an appointment with her physician. Make sure she calls her family doctor or primary physician. This is the doctor who should have the best overview of her entire medical history. If she is not able to make an office visit, the telephone will have to suffice.

Next you need to help her decide if she wants to do this her-

self or if she would rather have you with her to help her remember what the doctor said. She may have a relative she
would prefer to go with her to the doctor. Remember that one of
the cardinal rules of helping is never to do for people what they
can do for themselves or have other resources do for them.

Step three in this example is to make the office visit or telephone call. Then the two of you can talk about what the doctor
said to make sure that the woman understands what has been
said. Often it is helpful to have the doctor write down the information so that the woman can refresh her memory if she later
becomes confused or forgets.

During this entire referral process, you have been involved
as a support person but you have clearly stayed within the
bounds of doing what you know how to do.

Confidentiality

An extremely important part of helping and ministry is the way
in which helpers handle information to which they gained access during the helping process. When people who are being
helped tell you about themselves and their life situations, you
are bound by the rules of confidentiality. People to whom you
offer a helping/redemptive relationship begin to trust that you
care about them and have their best interests foremost in your
mind. Any information they give you then falls within the
bounds of confidentiality.

A policy on confidentiality should be established before a
problem arises. If you want help in developing your policy, ask
a social service agency for a copy of its policy on this subject and
adapt it for your situation. In addition, books on professional
helping are available at your local library. Most of these books
will include a section on the confidential handling of client information.

Confidentiality does not, however, mean total secrecy.
Never promise people that you will not tell anyone what they
say. Confidentiality requires that you reveal information if not
telling may cause serious physical or emotional harm to the person or to someone else. In this case, you can relay information
only after you have made reasonable effort to tell the person involved that you are going to reveal the information to appropriate people or officials. For example, a person with whom you
are ministering tells you that he is going to commit suicide. In

this situation, you cannot remain silent about this knowledge. You must try to get help for him. In such an instance, you need to tell his doctor, mental health worker, or some member of his family. If a young child relates to you that she is going to run away from home, you must inform the family after telling the child that you plan to do so.

It is appropriate to share information with other helpers involved. For example, if you learn that a parent of the child you are helping in an afterschool adventure club has recently been incarcerated, it is appropriate to share this information with the other volunteers working with this same club. This will enable them to be more sensitive to the needs of this particular child. This kind of sharing is permissible because the other volunteers are bound by the same policy of confidentiality as you are. If in your judgment there is no compelling reason to tell the other volunteers a piece of information you have, do not.

In a situation in which a piece of information will not likely cause harm to the person involved or another person, you must not share the information with uninvolved people. Use your best judgment to determine this. Examples of information that you cannot share include a person telling you that her marriage is in trouble or a father telling you the amount of money he earns each pay period.

One way to think about confidentiality in helping is to think of the confidentiality agreements you have with your physician, your attorney, or your pastor. These people are bound by the legal rules of privileged information. While as volunteers we are not legally bound by the rules of privileged information, we are to act as if we are for several reasons. People will not tell us what we need to know to help unless they trust us. And if they are to trust us, we must be trustworthy. People as beings of worth and dignity have a right to privacy, and in a sense helping is an intrusion into that right to privacy. A cardinal rule of helping is to limit this intrusion as much as possible. Helpers should limit their need to know to those things that are essential to help the client access the services the helpers are offering.

However, when we offer to help, we of necessity learn things that we would not have otherwise known. For example, if a child is referred to you for tutoring, you now have a piece of critical information about this child. He or she is a poor reader. You would never have known this fact other than through offering to help. If a person you help cannot trust that you will hold information in sacred trust, she may not feel comfortable enough later to come to your church for fear that you have told everyone all about her before she arrives. Shame is a powerful inhibitor of human motivation.

Confidentiality covers not only verbal information but written, taped, or electronically stored information. For example, you lead a group to help young mothers learn parenting skills. You want to take some slides to show to the larger group of the sponsoring church. You will need to get permission from the mothers in the club before you take pictures of them that will be shown to others outside the group. In addition, notes, files, and attendance charts should not be left out on desk tops where other people can read them. Personal information stored in computer files should be protected with passwords known only to those bound by your policy of confidentiality.

Addresses, telephone numbers, ages, and any other demographic data must also be held in trust. It is inappropriate to simply turn these names, addresses, and telephone numbers over to the church prospect committee. Think for a moment what you would think if your physician gave your name and phone number to a visitation committee from a local church. The only circumstance under which you could give the names and phone numbers of these mothers to a church is with the permission of the mothers.

One closing word about confidentiality relates to praying in public. People who offer public prayers must also respect a person's right to privacy and confidentiality. Prayer meetings are often places of violation of people's right to privacy. Just because you are praying for people at Wednesday night prayer meeting does not mean you need to make public everything about the life situation of the person for whom you are praying. For example, recently I heard a prayer for a woman who was having difficulty. The person offering the prayer named the person and the institution. All of us hearing knew that this institution was a detoxification program for people who are chemically dependent. I did not need to know that this woman was chemically dependent in order to remember her in prayer; God certainly already knew. I like the policies that some churches have of not listing people on the prayer list without their permission. This shows great sensitivity and respect for hurting people.

Summary

The principles of helping discussed in this chapter have been drawn from the model of the ministry of Jesus, both explicit and implicit, and the literature of the helping professions. It is only a beginning point for you. As you minister and witness to others, keep these guidelines in mind.

1. You are a part of a larger helping network in your community. Connect with this network and, in so doing, help make it stronger and more user friendly to people who need its help. Make referrals to other parts of this network. They are your allies.

2. Information you receive in the process of helping is a sacred trust. Handle this information with confidentiality.

3. Become a lifelong learner. Every day try to learn at least one new thing about helping. The library is full of books that will help you become a more effective helper and minister.

4. Work to increase your competency in offering helping/redemptive relationships to people. Practice acting out the characteristics of this kind of relationship with others.

5. Daily take stock of your limitations and learn to be honest about what you can do or cannot do. Try never to go beyond your competencies.

6. Be real. Daily work on closing any gaps that exist between what you believe and how you act.

Learning Activities

1. Think about the kind of helping relationship you have been offering to people. How did you learn to relate in the way you now do? Think about who taught you to care about people.

2. Decide if you need to change some aspect of your current helping relationship patterns. How would you rate yourself in each of the elements of the helping/redemptive relationship that Jesus offers to us? Make a list of these elements. Pick one on which you will begin to work. Plan a way to monitor

your progress. What role do you think prayer will play in your effort to change?

3. What is the difference in priestly and prophetic helping? Which of these is easier for you to do? Do you know why this is true? Try to help in the way that is less comfortable for you. What did you learn about yourself in the process?

4. What is a referral? Write out your response in your own words. What is meant by the statement in this chapter that we are all a part of the helping network? Do you agree or disagree? Why?

5. If your community has a resource directory, secure a copy. Study the volume to familiarize yourself with the helping network. List three new services you discover in your community.

6. Review the list of the information needed to make a referral outlined in this chapter. Call two of the new services you discovered and see if you can secure the information needed to make referrals to these agencies.

7. What is meant by confidentiality? Are you able to keep information about others as a sacred trust? Have you thought about the role this factor plays in the helping process? Will you be more conscious of it in the future?

8. Listen more closely to public prayers in the future. See if you find evidence to support the author's claim that confidentiality is sometimes violated in public prayers. Check with your church to see if there are policies regulating how names are added to the prayer list. Are you satisfied with these policies? What changes might you recommend?

---

* Women on Mission is the WMU organization for women aged 18 and up. For more information, call 1 (800) 968-7301.

4

Who Needs a Neighbor?

They stood at the door of the Baptist center. The young man and young woman were both in their early 30s. Their faces were filled with anxiety, and their bodies seemed to sag. I knew something bad had happened.

I met them two years earlier as I was visiting in the community. After numerous visits a relationship developed among us, and they began coming to weekday programs at the center. She enrolled in a Mothers' Club; he came to family night activities. Both had been Christians for a number of years and soon joined the small fellowship that worshiped on Sunday and Wednesday nights in the center building.

They had been married for 10 years and had lived all of their married life in a small, three-room house nearby. Their three children were all under 8 years of age. The oldest son was in school, and the woman took care of the younger son and daughter at home. The husband worked as a sign painter for a local tobacco warehouse where he earned minimum wage. The mother, when she had time, made doll clothes and sold them on the street to earn extra income.

Despite their best efforts, they were poor. They lived in substandard housing; they had no health insurance. Most of their clothes came from the clothing program at the center. Each day was a struggle as they tried to pay their bills and feed their family. On several occasions, they borrowed money from the center lending fund, always repaying the loan before the due date.

After I opened the door and invited them into the foyer, the woman told me they had a problem. When we sat down to talk, the man kept his eyes focused on the floor. It seemed that the trouble began at work. Although he was a sign painter, he could not read nor write . . . a fact he hid from his boss because he was afraid of the consequences. But the boss found out and told the man that if he wanted to keep his job, he had to learn to read and write.

As their story unraveled, the young man began to lift his head a little. He was a good sign painter. In days past he had shown me some of his work. How, I thought, could you be a sign painter and not be able to read and write? But together, the couple had managed. Every afternoon before he left work, he would ask his boss what signs he would need to paint the following day. He did this, he told his boss, so he could come early in the mornings and work. The young man would go home and tell his wife, who could read and write, how the signs were to read. Using her skills, she would write out what had to go on the signs. He would then memorize the shapes and spaces. In other words, he was painting the signs as you or I would draw a tree or a flower. The next day, he would go back and paint the signs. This all went well for a long time. However, on this particular day, the boss changed his mind about the lettering he wanted on the sign. When he told this sign painter, the young man had no choice but to reveal his problem to the boss. Now the two of them had come asking if I knew of anyone who could teach him how to read.

Hawks and Swans

They came as a group. I heard them long before I saw them, these teenagers from the local high school. I knew them from having worked with them in two clubs, the Hawks for the boys and the Swans for the girls. The clubs had been started at a local mission when most of these youth were between 11 and 12 years old. Now they were 17 and 18 years old.

To my knowledge no one in any of the families represented in the two groups had ever completed high school. One of the goals of the clubs was to give these young people the encouragement and support they needed to stay in school. With one or two exceptions, all of the more than 20 youth involved had stayed in school.

On that particular day, the local high school had announced the plan for the junior/senior class trip to Washington, D. C. When the cost of going on the trip was announced, it was obvious to the Hawks and Swans that none of them could afford to go. Later talks with their parents confirmed this. To say that they were disappointed would be an understatement.

Here they came with long faces and deferred dreams. They had come to the mission because it was the place they had come to identify as a place of hope. After I invited them in, their story came tumbling out. They wanted to go on a junior/senior trip. They wanted to have something to talk about at school. They wanted to be like their peers. They were tired of being poor. They were weary of not being able to do what other teenagers did. Their intense eyes said they were poor and could do nothing to change their life situations. They came asking for a chance to realize a dream.

Caregiver

She sat across the table from me in a local social service agency. She was an attractive woman who appeared to be in her late 60s. She was well dressed and from all indications seemed to be financially affluent. She was well educated and spoke with polish. However, she looked tired and frustrated. She began to cry, and it was as if the tears that had been held back for so long could no longer be restrained. She sobbed.

Her story was slow in coming. It was hard for her to tell anyone what her life was like. Married at a young age, she and her husband had recently celebrated their golden anniversary. They had one son who lived about 2,000 miles away and had a family of his own. She rarely saw him. About ten years before, her mother had become disabled and had moved in with her and her husband. At first things went along fairly well. But as time passed, her mother became increasingly hard to manage. Recently, her mother's physician told her that her mother had Alzheimer's disease.

"How am I going to care for Mother?" she asked. It seemed that the woman's two brothers were not going to be much help. One said that he could not stand seeing his mother in this condition. The other was married and his wife was ill also. It was all he could do to take care of her. The woman felt guilty at the thought of putting her mother in a nursing facility, but what else could she do? She said her husband was growing increasingly impatient with her. He had worked hard all his life and now in his retirement, he wanted to travel and enjoy a more carefree life with her.

She continued to sob as she said she felt caught between the demands of her husband and the responsibility to care for her mother. She loved both these people and wanted to do what was right. The situation was tearing her apart. She was depressed and felt like she could not go on living this way. She just wanted to run away from it all. She had been able to handle life's problems up until this time, but this was just too much. She would be glad to pay what the agency charged if only there were someone who could help her get back control of her life so she could make some decisions.

Single Mother

The call from a neighbor came early one morning. The house across the street from the church was on fire. I knew the single mother and her three children who lived there. When I arrived on the scene, there was nothing left of the little shotgun house but ashes and pieces of twisted wiring. She stood off to the side with the three children huddled around her. Tears of utter despair streamed down her face. She had struggled so hard to live on the minimum wage she earned working at a nearby fast-food restaurant. Before going to work each day, she would get the children ready and walk them to a neighborhood day-care center. Then she would go home and get herself ready and walk to work.

Several months earlier when one of the children became ill, she had been forced to give up this job and go on welfare. The day care would not let the ill child attend. Though she called everyone she could think of, she could not find anyone to keep the child while she worked. Unable to find any alternative, she quit her job to care for the child. Her social worker had helped her get on food stamps.

In our conversations, she lamented the fact that she had no family to whom she could turn. Her mother was still alive but in ill health herself. Her father died several years ago. She said she had never intended to be a single mom but that one day her husband "just up and left." At the time she was glad he was gone because he had hit her the night before and she was afraid he would hurt the children. She was working to get him to pay child support, but the authorities had not been able to determine his whereabouts.

Now she stood beside the ashes with the three children

huddled around her while tears stream down her cheeks. No call for help came from her lips; she was beyond even asking.

Each of these vignettes represents real people. As I recall their life situations, their faces flood my consciousness. I can still call them all by name. Jesus made it clear in Luke 10:36–37 that a neighbor is one who shows mercy to people such as these. Because some Christians in Elkhorn Baptist Association in Kentucky took this instruction seriously, lives were touched and mercy was shown.

A member of a local church's Woman's Missionary Union taught the sign painter to read. I remember their times together over a kitchen table as he learned to sound out the letters and slowly began to read "cup" and "bird." He came one day to show me that he could now write his name.

The Hawks and the Swans set up an employment agency with local churches and earned enough money raking leaves, cleaning windows, and doing other odd jobs to pay for their own trip to Washington, D. C. As I rode through our nation's capital on a tour bus with a large "Hawks and Swans" sign on its side, I knew the lives of these teenagers would never be the same. They all graduated from high school, two went on to college, and one earned a PhD.

The woman who was caring for her mother with Alzheimer's disease received counseling and was able to make the necessary choices for the good of herself and her family. The caregiving role did not go away for a long time, but she found a support group for caregivers of people with Alzheimer's at a local church. She was later able to face the fact that she could not care for her mother at home. The mother was placed in a Baptist gerontological facility equipped to care for Alzheimer's patients.

Someone found a place for the single mom and her children to live. A member of a local church helped her to get a job which paid a decent wage, and she was able to keep her family together. A lawyer from a local Brotherhood group helped her locate her ex-husband and he was forced to begin child support payments. A group began to work on legislation to present to the state house and senate to make absent fathers more accountable for the support of their children. These Christians were neighbors because they showed mercy to people in need.

With these witness and ministry examples fresh in our minds, remember the poor and vulnerable groups to whom Christ ministered. The question now is, Who are the groups of people living near us who need mercy? Who are the people today needing to be ministered to by others who are following the witness and ministry model of Jesus?

The groups that represent the vulnerable groups to which Jesus ministered are numerous. To discuss the life situations of each of these groups would take several volumes. Only six groups will be singled out here for discussion. These six, which serve as examples of the larger population, are people who live in poverty, people who experience homelessness, special needs subgroups of the elderly population, people who cannot read or write, individuals and families who are victims of violence, and families and victims affected by human immunodeficiency virus (HIV) or acquired immune deficiency syndrome (AIDS).

People Who Live in Poverty

Just as in Jesus' time, many people today are poor. However, in my 45 years of ministry, I have not met one person who liked living in poverty. For the last five decades, the percentage of people living in poverty in America has hovered around 15 percent of the total population. Every community has people who suffer from the pain and devastation of being poor.

On July 1, 1995, there were 262.8 million people living in the United States. The US Census Bureau predicts that by the year 2050 the nation's population will rise to 393.9 million. Based on this estimate of 15 percent, in 1996 about 40 million people in the United States live in poverty. These data also indicate that unless we do something to change this trend and if the population projections hold true, that by the year 2050 more than 59 million people will be experiencing this tragic life situation.

Definitions of Poverty

In order to understand what these figures and percentages mean, poverty has to be defined. The authors of *Child Poverty in America* define it in terms of life situations. For these writers a family is poor when they have to "constantly choose between paying the rent or the heat or electric bill, between buying food or replacing the children's worn out shoes, between keeping up with the doctors' bills or fixing the car that is needed to go to and from work."[8]

In a more technical sense, poverty in the United States is defined by the amount of money it takes for different size families to sustain a minimum standard of living. This definition is generally referred to as "the official poverty line." In 1964, when the national administration was working on the War on Poverty program structure, Social Security Administration employee Mollie Orshanksy and her staff developed a formula to calculate the "official poverty line." In more recent years, the official poverty line amounts have been determined and reported by the US Census Bureau.

Orshanksy determined, with the help of the Department of Agriculture, what it would cost families ranging from one member to nine or more to purchase food for a minimally adequate diet for a year. Earlier Department of Agriculture studies had revealed that the average low-income family spent one-third of its budget on food. Using this information, Orshanksy multiplied the cost of the minimal adequate diet by a factor of three. The resulting figure became the official poverty line. Families with income below this line were poor; those above this line were not. Different amounts were calculated for families based primarily on the number of people living in the family.[9] Each year since, the poverty line has been figured and adjusted according to the changes in the Consumer Price Index. For example, in 1994 a family of four in the United States whose income was less than $15,286 was considered to be living in poverty.

A poverty line of $15,286 for a family of four, assuming that a low-income family spends one-third of its income for food, means that the family can be expected to spend $5,095 for food. A family of four eating three meals a day for a year consumes 4,380 meals. Simple arithmetic shows that this allows for an expenditure of approximately $1.16 per person per meal. What kind of meal would you prepare for four people which cost only $4.64 in 1994 dollars. When the numbers are examined at this level, the true nature of poverty becomes obvious.

Another way of looking at the poverty line is to note that if a person worked fulltime (40 hours a week) in 1995 at minimum wage, that person's annual income would have amounted to

$8,840 before taxes. This income would have fallen $5,406 short of the official poverty line. Full-time employment at minimum wage for one person still leaves a family of four in poverty. In order to meet the 1994 official line of poverty for a four-member family, a wage earner had to earn at least $7.35 per hour and work 40 hours a week. By 1996, this figure rose to approximately $7.50 per hour.

"Going on welfare" is not an answer to poverty. Aid to Families with Dependent Children (AFDC) payments for a mother and three children in Kentucky were $285 dollars a month in 1995. Nineteen years ago payments were $235. In other words, while the cost of living during those 19 years increased by 300 percent, the AFDC payments increased by only 17.5 percent.

According to a Louisville Coalition for the Homeless Report, even combined with food stamps and health care coverage, AFDC does not provide enough money for a family in Kentucky to rise above the poverty line. As this manuscript is being prepared, welfare reform legislation is before Congress. The outcome of this legislation is unknown at this time.

People Who Are at High Risk to Become Poor

Some groups in our society are more likely to be poor than others. African Americans are three times more likely to be poor than Anglos. Mother-only families are five times more likely to be poor than two-parent families. Families in which the bread winner has no more than 8 years of schooling are almost five times more likely to be poor than families in which the chief earner has a college education. Children are more likely to be poor than older adults. The number of children under 6 years of age who grow up in poor families increased from 3.4 million in 1972 to 6 million in 1992. Little has been done since then to change this trend. Another 9.7 million children and youth between the ages of 6 and 18 are poor.

Mother-only families in the United States are at special risk of being poor. In fact, they are at greater risk if they live in the United States than if the live in any other western industrialized nation. For example, in 1991, 53 percent of mother-only families in the United States were poor as compared to 45 percent in Canada, 18 percent in the United Kingdom, and 16 percent in France

While the risk of senior adults becoming poor is less than it was 25 years ago, there are still many senior adults, especially in the 85- to 100-year-old group, who live in poverty. Those in this age group who are at the greatest risk are the frail elderly. Social Security payments, Supplemental Security Income, Medicare, private pensions, and veterans' pensions have greatly reduced this risk. However, this group still comprised 3 million of the 39.3 million people who lived in poverty in America in 1993. If these older adults have survived all the members of their family, then they are at an even higher risk of being poor.

Another group at risk of being poor includes people who are unable to get a job because of personal challenges, physical or mental illnesses, responsibilities of caring for young children or aging parents, or scarcity of jobs. (Scarcity of jobs can either mean that jobs which pay enough to rise above poverty are not available or that persons are not trained to fill the available jobs that do pay enough.)

The phenomenon of "mistraining" has become more of a problem as America has shifted from a manufacturing economy to a service-oriented economy. In President Clinton's Educational Technology Initiative, Vice-President Al Gore noted that by the year 2000 a majority of the new jobs created in the United States will "require advanced technological skills." The majority of people presently unemployed in America do not now have, nor will they likely be trained in, the technological skills needed to be hired in the majority of the new jobs projected between now and the year 2000. While unemployment among American civilian workers decreased from 7.2 percent in 1985 to 5.6 percent in 1995, this still leaves significant numbers of workers looking for employment but unable to find it.

In summary then, people who are at greatest risk of being poor are African Americans, children, youth, mother-only families, primary wage earners paid the minimum wage, full-time employees with less than 8 years of education, and the unemployed or unemployable. Another way to summarize the data is to ask, "Who are poor because they don't want to work?" Take out a piece of paper and let's see. Start with the 39.3 million people in the United States who were living in poverty 1993. Put this figure in a column entitled "People

Who Are Poor." Start another column, entitled "People Who Cannot Work." In this second column put the 6 million children under 6 years of age who are poor, the 3 million older adults who are poor, the 9.7 million youth between the ages of 6 and 18 years old who are poor, the 15.7 million people who worked fulltime and still could not overcome poverty, and the 2.2 million who are looking for work and cannot find a job for which they are trained. Also remember that we have not accounted for those who are unemployed because they are disabled or because they have to stay home and care for small children or aging parents. Estimate this at about another million. Add up the second column and subtract the total from the first column figure. This leaves about 1.7 million in all other categories of people who live in poverty, or 4.3 percent of those people who were poor in 1993. If we made everyone work who was employable, 95.7 percent of those people who were poor would still need income supplements. These are 1993 figures; however, there is no evidence to indicate that this will change anytime soon. As you can see, people are not poor because they do not want to work. The causes are much more complex.

People who are not poor often have a problem helping people who are poor. The assumption on the part of many of the 85 percent who are not poor is that anyone who wants to get out of poverty can if he or she is willing to work hard enough and wants to badly enough. The above figures should dispel this notion.

People Who Are Homeless

"'Give me your tired, your poor, Your huddled masses yearning to breath free. . . . Send these, the homeless, tempest-tost to me, I lift my lamp beside the golden door.'" When I first read this line from Emma Lazarus's "The New Colossus," I only thought of the immigrants as they first caught sight of the Statue of Liberty upon arrival in America. Who would have thought of them as homeless? Of course there were always a few transient men who stayed in the rescue missions in large cities, but in the 1960s most Americans had homes to live in, albeit that some of these houses in rural areas and city centers were substandard.

This all changed beginning in the late 1970s. In 1985 Brian Kates, a reporter for the *New York Daily News*, wrote a book entitled *The Murder of a Shopping Bag Lady*. The subject of the story was Phyllis Iannotta, who "spent her first birthday aboard the SS *Stampalia* en route to Ellis Island." She was murdered in a parking lot in New York's Hell's Kitchen. For 50 years she had supported herself. The book is a review of Kates's investigation of how the bureaucratic maze moved Phyllis from being self-supporting to being homeless. Other books were written and other newspaper stories printed. Homeless advocates started educating the public about the problem.

By the mid-1980s, the sheer numbers of homeless in American had grown so dramatically that their presence in public facilities and on the streets made the country aware that something was badly wrong. It is rare that a social problem of the magnitude of homelessness happens so quickly. In a short time communities everywhere were opening emergency shelters. By the early 1990s the word *emergency* was dropped and they were simply called shelters. The shelters had been around for over a decade and they had become permanent fixtures. However, there never seemed to be enough to give everyone a place to stay. The homeless now included working families whose income was too low to afford rent, deinstitutionalized people who suffered from mental disorders, families who had lost their farms and farm workers who were displaced, spouses who were being battered, mother-only families with children, and single women with no means of support all joined the more traditional homeless clientele—the transient men.

Scope and Definitions of Homelessness

No one knows exactly how many people in the United States are homeless. The National Coalition for the Homeless in Washington, D. C., claims that the difficulty in determining the number of homeless is caused primarily by the logistics of finding and counting people who have no permanent address. Also, the social scientists who tabulate these counts use different definitions and methodologies. One way to define the homeless is the literal count of people who are living in shelters or on the street for one given day or one given week. This definition is called a point-in-time count. According to a 1996 National Coalition for the Homeless fact sheet, a study by Martha Burt and Barbara Cohen used a point-in-time count to estimate that between 500,000 and 600,000 people were homeless.

Another way to define the homeless is to interview a sample of the general population and ask them if there was ever a time when they considered themselves to be homeless. This figure then is used to estimate the number of homeless. This method is called the period-prevalence count. Based on this methodology, the number of homeless people is estimated by the Department of Housing and Urban Development as ranging around 7 million. Regardless of which estimate you consider, it is obvious that many Americans experience homelessness.

Causes of Homelessness

The sharp rise in the incidents of homelessness has many complex causes. Anyone who lived in rental property in the 1980s can attest to the sharp rise in rental cost. In many instances, rent doubled in the decade between 1980 and 1990, simply pricing many people out of the rental market. In addition to this rise in cost, low-income rental properties decreased in number. Some rental units in low-income areas were lost through normal wear and tear. Many were lost through "gentrification" and urban renewal. Many cities tore down whole low-income neighborhoods to build high-priced condominiums, upscale rental units, or sports arenas. Many young professionals began to move back to the city.

Whole areas of structurally sound low-income houses were bought at low cost. These older, large houses had been turned into three or four apartments. They were remodeled and became single or, at most, two-family dwellings. The low-income families who had lived in these houses could not afford the new rent or compete for the purchase and reclaiming of these houses. They were displaced, and if they were not fortunate enough to find other affordable housing in a tight market, they became homeless.

The stock of decent and affordable housing in the United States has decreased during the last decade. Builders found greater profits in building suburban homes for middle- and upper-income level people. Little new affordable housing was built in the city or in rural areas. Money was not made available for building houses because banks "red-lined" these areas, becoming more and more reluctant to invest money in high-risk areas where low-income people lived.

Chemical dependency is also a problem that increases the number of homeless people. Shelter workers report a high incidence of alcoholism and other forms of chemical dependency among those who come to shelters. This is particularly true of single men. However, it should be noted that where no long-term programs of drug rehabilitation are available, people with this problem have no place to go but to homeless shelters. This is especially true when the temperature drops below freezing in winter or rises above safety levels in summer.

Another reason for the sharp increase in homelessness was the sharp drop in the level of real income for blue-collar and unskilled workers. The move away from a primarily manufacturing economy to a service economy also left many blue-collar and unskilled workers without jobs. Factories closed, business merged, and companies downsized.

Prior to the 1970s, many people who experienced homelessness simply doubled up. They moved in with family or friends until they could find some other solution. As homelessness became a more chronic than acute problem, this solution became less tenable. The longer the person was homeless, the harder it became to find some other family with whom to double up. These crowded conditions did not prove manageable. For example, a 1994 study by a Coalition for the Homeless task force in Louisville, Kentucky, revealed that 19.6 percent of the respondents stated overcrowding where they last lived as their reason for being homeless.

The 1980s also witnessed changing attitudes toward child and spouse abuse. More women and their children who were being abused decided that being beaten and permanently injured were too high a price to pay just to have a roof over their heads. They sought refuge in shelters and centers with services to women and families.

Many who lived in institutional care in what used to be called state mental hospitals and in other facilities that care for persons with mental illnesses were released through deinstitutionalization programs in the early 1970s. This program of getting people out of state mental hospitals and back into their communities was a sound one. People need to be helped in the least restrictive environments. However, in order to do this, local mental health centers and other needed support services were to be provided in every community to help these individuals sustain themselves. The supports were never fully funded. Most communities developed only partial support that fell far short of what was needed. Many who were released from the hospitals eventually joined the ranks of the homeless.

All these factors combined to make homelessness a life situation for many people. While any one or two of these problem situations could have been absorbed, they all happened too close together for society to respond. The greater tragedy is that American society has not yet responded with any permanent solution, and the problem of homelessness increases with each passing year.

It is hard for a middle-class American Christian who has never been in danger of being homeless to know what it means. Some Christians have observed homelessness by serving in soup kitchens, shelters, and rescue missions. However, the life situation of the homeless person or family is still foreign to most church members. In 1993 Elliot Liebow wrote a book called, *Tell Them Who I Am: The Lives of Homeless Women.* He began with the intention of writing a descriptive analysis of what life was like for women living in three shelters in Washington, D. C. However, in the process of getting to know the women, he shifted his aim to trying to communicate to his readership how these women "were able to remain human in such an inhumane environment" where they were considered "surplus people." The homeless populations of our nation need neighbors.

Subgroups Within the Elderly Population
Many older persons are able to take care of themselves. In recent years, with the help of Social Security, Supplemental Security Income, and retirement benefits, many senior citizens are no longer living in poverty. Numbers of older people have families and friends who provide the social support networks that enable them to live quality lives in their own homes. However, subgroups within this larger population group need assistance and people who will be neighbors to them.

An exhaustive list of these subgroups cannot be presented here. However, for the purposes of this book, several examples will be presented to illustrate the needs of the older adult subgroups. Perhaps these will demonstrate the magnitude of the needs involved.

Frail Elderly Who Still Live in Their Own Homes

Within the last decade, the use of "old" to describe people over 65 years of age had lost its usefulness. The needs and life situations of people who are in their 60s and early 70s are generally very different from the growing numbers of people who are living till their late 80s and 90s.

While there are exceptions, the frail elderly are likely to be 85 years old or older. According to N. R. Hooyman and H. A. Kiyak in their book *Social Gerontology*, a high percentage of the frail elderly are women, and an increasing number of these women will be members of ethnic groups. The May 1996 White House Conference on Aging reported that "minority elderly will double by the year 2030." This same report also focused on "the rapid growth in the number of older women." Women, especially women members of minority groups, are at risk of becoming poor.

The typical needs of the frail elderly who still live in their own homes are for congregate or home-delivered meals; transportation; home safety checks; home health care; social interaction networks; and assistance in maintaining health through exercise, diet, and good habits of personal care. In addition, often they will need help in accessing local human services and other helping resources available to them. They will be able to continue living in their own homes only if family, friends, and neighbors regularly check on them and help out when needed.

Senior Adult Caregivers

In recent years, senior adults have become a primary source of caregivers in this country. Two primary areas of caregiving focus on caring for children and aging parents.

Currently grandparents have primary responsibility for more than 3 million grandchildren in the United States. The reasons for this growing need for grandparents to care for children include parents who abandon their children because of drug abuse, parents who are homeless due to poverty, and the death or illness of one or both parents.

Whatever the cause, senior adults are being called on to be primary caregivers for a substantial number of American children.

The number of people in their 70s who are primary caregivers for their parents who are in their 90s continues to rise. Family members are still viewed as the primary caregivers for older adults. Only 5 percent of the older adults who live in the United States, at any given time, are in institutions such as nursing homes. While most of these 70-year-olds are more than willing to care for their parents, they are often not physically or economically able to carry this load. This kind of caregiving requires constant attention to the needs of the aging parent. Just when the 70-year-olds are in a position to assist their own children and carry the normal grandparent roles, they find themselves confined at home to care for their own parents. Even when the parent(s) are in a skilled nursing facility, there are regular demands on adult children to visit and assist with the monitoring and care of their parents.

It is easy to understand why this generation of the "young" old have been called the sandwich generation. They are indeed caught between two generations, both of whom need them as caregivers. As the number of people who live to reach their late 90s increases and as young families in America are increasingly at risk, this role of caregiver for older adults will increasingly become a stress-producing life situation.

Another population issue will influence this caregiver role as well. In the years of the Great Depression and the decade which followed, there was a major drop in the number of births in this country. This means that the number of people now living between the ages of 50 to 66 is smaller than in other generations. There will be fewer of them to carry the caregiver role for their older parents, their baby boomer children, and their grandchildren.

Older adults who have significant caregiving responsibilities need neighbors. This group needs some respite time. They need other people who will run some of the errands, make some of the visits, look after the children on occasion, sit with their parents one morning a week, and listen to their stories when the stress and strain of giving care to others becomes overwhelming.

Older Adults Who Need Guardians

In the May 1995 issues of *NASW News*, the American Bar Association reported that there were an estimated 400,000 to 500,000 older Americans who have most of their decisions made for them by court appointed guardians. Every state, as well as the District of Columbia, has mechanisms by which courts can appoint such guardians for older adults who need them. In 1978, the American Bar Association established a Commission on Legal Problems of the Elderly. This commission includes lawyers, judges, physicians, professors, aging network leaders, and advocates. Its purpose is to examine the laws relating to concerns of the aging population. They have focused on legal issues related to long-term care, surrogate decision making, individual rights, guardianship, housing, Social Security, and other public benefit programs.

Sometimes older adults become unable to make most of the decisions related to their care and assets. In these situations, the courts, while protecting the individual rights of the older adult, must appoint a guardian. This court-appointed guardian may or may not be someone who knows the older adult involved. People are needed to serve in this role of guardian. Perhaps church members can fill this gap.

Older Women in Poverty

As early as 1988, the Senate Special Committee on Aging reported that almost 75 percent of the elderly poor in this country are women. Women over 65 years of age are twice as likely to be poor as men in this same age cohort. This growing problem is discussed in-depth earlier in this chapter.

People Who Cannot Read and Write

On my guest bedroom wall hangs a beautifully matted and framed family treasure: two canceled checks. One of the checks was written to pay for my paternal grandmother's grave stone. The other one was written in payment for a refrigerator which my paternal grandfather bought for her some years earlier. The reason I saved them, however, is not because of why they were written but because of how they were written. On each of them there is a small X. Along side the X is my grandfather's name and the person who witnessed his X. I loved him dearly and liked to talk to him. I remember how much he loved homemade ice cream. He would eat it until he got so cold that he would put on a heavy coat and keep eating! He never learned to read and write.

The beginning of the modern literacy movement grew out of the discovery that about one-third of the men inducted into service during World War I were not able to read and write well enough to make them effective soldiers. At the start of the war, my grandfather was 40 years old, so you see he was not alone.

According to the 1996 *Grolier Multimedia Encyclopedia*, the phrase *functional literacy* was coined to describe those people who could not read and write well enough to function effectively in society. Functional literacy is usually categorized into three types. Cultural literacy is the "ability to read in order to express oneself, solve problems, and participate in an educated society." Critical literacy is "reading not just for information but to evaluate that information." Workplace literacy involves the ability to read and write to a level required by a given job. This may include the ability to use a computer, read designs, or follow written instructions.

In a more practical sense, functional illiteracy is the inability to read a newspaper, follow instructions on medicines, read street signs, or shop if the selection of a product requires reading. In an article in the Kentucky Baptist Convention's newsjournal *Western Recorder*, Joyce Sweeney Martin noted that there are about 27 million people in the United States who are not functionally literate and about 45 million more who are "only marginally competent" in their reading and writing skills.

The largest segment of this population is made up of native-born adults who never learned to read and write. A smaller percentage includes adults for whom English is a second language. A third group, school youth who cannot read and write, has received much national publicity during the last two decades.

People who are not literate are often shut out of the market place. Today the only jobs available to them are ones involving menial or seasonal labor which, in most cases, will not pay enough to support the workers or their families. Employers have recognized the impact of this problem on the labor force. If people are to be able to fill the new jobs being developed in the United States, they will have to be able to read and write at a higher than 12th-grade level.

On a personal level, the cost of illiteracy is extremely high. The pain of struggling to live and feed a family, the stress of not being able to help children with homework, or the loss of self-esteem at work are just a few of these personal costs. However, there are societal costs as well. Grolier's encyclopedia states that the economic and social costs of illiteracy in the United States are about $200 billion dollars annually. The cost to persons and to the nation are too high to ignore.

Victims of Violence

No case needs to be made to convince us that violence is a problem in our society. Our newspapers and televisions daily relate the life situations of victims of violence in our neighborhoods, across the country, and around the world. It is a problem which impacts every community and church congregation. Violence on the streets, violence resulting from hate crimes, and violence in families are of grave concern to most people in our country. Children, women, and the frail elderly are the most likely victims of family violence. Victims of hate crimes are usually members of ethnic or racial groups. Victims of street violence are generally youth living in the central city or bystanders who just happen to be in the wrong place at the wrong time.

Battered Women

In the last 20 years, there has been an increasing awareness of the extent and intensity of the assaults on female victims of family violence. Annually millions of women in the United States are physically or psychologically battered by their spouses or their boyfriends. Most experts claim that severe physical abuse of women occurs in about 10 percent of all marriages and that in about 65 percent of these marriages the abuse is recurring.[10] Often these assaults take place after the perpetrator has used alcohol or some type of illegal drug.

Women initially tend to stay in the abusive situation because they think there is something they can do to change the situation and thus stop the abuse. Even when women recognize that this is a fantasy, they are often afraid to leave because the perpetrator has threatened to do greater harm if they press charges or move out. Many jurisdictions now require law enforcement officials to arrest persons in cases of probable wife beating whether or not the wife files a complaint. This has taken the wife out of the role of accuser and makes her less vulnerable. In cases that involve children, the woman is often economically dependent on the abusive spouse and afraid to leave because she does not know how she will feed and otherwise care for her children.

Many women who suffered abuse testify that they left home when they knew that if they stayed their spouse would kill them or their children. The evidence in the daily newspapers attests to the reality of their fears. Husbands manage to kill their estranged wives and children even when the courts have issued emergency protective orders designed to keep perpetrators a safe distance away.

In the early 1970s, programs to provide shelter and care for abused women and their children began to be established. In 1984, Congress passed the Family Violence Prevention and Services Act. This legislation authorized money to be sent to the states to develop programs to prevent family violence and to provide emergency services to the victims of family violence. In addition it funded training and technical assistance to prepare people to help the victims.

While much has been done to prevent family violence, it still stands as one of the major problems for women and children in the United States. Women who are abused and children who live in homes where their mother is being beaten or otherwise abused by their father are in need of helping neighbors. While care must be taken in such dangerous situations, there are ways to help which are safe and redemptive.

Child Abuse Victims

I shall never forget the first abused child with whom I worked. The 18-month-old child had cigarette burns all over her hips and massive bruises over her arms and legs. It was a horrendous sight. It is hard to believe what adults will do to children. Today in this country the incidence of physical, sexual, and emotional abuse of children is rising. In 1990 the number of substantiated cases of child neglect and/or abuse was 801,143, noted a report from the US Department of Health and Human Services. By 1991 this figure rose to 819,922 cases, an increase of almost 19,000 children. This situation is intolerable.

Physical abuse of children may result in broken bones, unusual bruises not typical of falls, burns, and other flesh wounds. Emotional abuse generally involves humiliation or berating that terrorizes children. They are left with little positive regard for themselves and view the world through lenses of shame and doubt. Sexual abuse of children may involve a range of sexual behaviors from inappropriate fondling to rape. In each of these instances children are severely hurt and their future chances for normal growth and development are changed forever. In a study carried out by Judith McNew and Neil Abell and reported in the January 1995 issue of *Social Work*, the findings indicated that people who were abused as children suffered from posttraumatic stress symptomatology much like Vietnam veterans who have experienced war-related trauma on measures of intrusion avoidance, anger experience and expression, intimacy, and anxiety.

Causal theories usually fall into one of two categories. Those which say that child abuse is caused by defects in the personality of the abuser were more popular several decades ago. The other group says that the causes of child abuse are a combination of poverty, substance abuse, and violence in society. Abusers are troubled people, and often they have suffered from abuse themselves. Inability to parent, lack of resources, stress, and substance abuse on the part of parents, guardians, and other caregivers for children have added to the problem.

Children have a right to be able to trust the adults on whom they depend for protection and provision of basic human needs. Most states now require any citizen who has reasonable suspicions that a child is being neglected or abused to report such concerns to the child protective services agency in the state. If citizens suspect child abuse or neglect and do not report this to the proper authorities, the citizens are liable for criminal prosecution. To offer children less protection and care is unacceptable. Many of these children and youth need us to be their neighbors.

Rape Victims

The vast majority of rape victims are females. Rape is often considered the most underreported violent crime in America. Women hesitate to report rape because they fear no one will believe them. Historically, the attitude that a woman's dress or demeanor somehow contributed to such incidents has also caused some women to hesitate to report. Since the perpetrator often was known to the victim before the rape took place, the woman may be threatened with greater harm if she tells. Also, in the present judicial system in our country, it is hard for a woman to get a conviction of the man who raped her. The emotional cost of going to court is high. The thought of going through this stressful court appearance with the likelihood that nothing will be done silences many women.

In 1992, Libby Bergman carried out a survey of 631 students in midwestern high schools to determine how many had experienced sexual, physical, or verbal date violence. The study, reported in a January 1992 *Social Work* article, revealed that 15.5 percent of the female high school students completing the survey had experienced sexual violence while on a date. This percentage rose to 24.6 when the female students were asked if they had experienced either sexual or physical violence or both while on a date. The young women who attended suburban schools reported the highest incidence of date violence. Students in inner-city schools were second highest, with those from rural schools lowest. The findings of the study clearly indicated that sexual and physical violence is a significant problem within dating relationships, especially in high school.

Elderly Abuse Victims

With the increase in the number of frail elderly, there has come an increased pressure on children to care for their aging parents at home. Within the last two decades, there has been a growing awareness that a number of these frail elderly are being abused by their own adult children or other family members or caregivers.

In response to this problem, most states have established laws to protect the welfare of the elderly. Adult protective services laws require that people who suspect that an older adult is being abused report this to the local authorities or to adult protective services workers. However, these laws do not prevent all cases of neglect or abuse of older people in our society.

This abuse generally takes the form of physical abuse or neglect. Older persons have been found locked in rooms, badly beaten, or undernourished with increasing frequency. Again this is an intolerable situation. These people need us to be their neighbors.

Victims of Hate Crime Violence

Acts of violence against people or organizations because of their race, ethnicity, religion, and/or other personal characteristics or life situations are defined as hate crimes. Arson of homes and businesses, harassment at homes or places of employment, destruction of church property or symbols of worship, and attacks on people are all examples of hate crimes.

Such crimes are not new to our world. African-American people have suffered from hate crimes since being brought to America as slaves. History is replete with this kind of violence against the Jewish people since biblical times. We all know stories of people who have had to leave their homes and move to other parts of the city to avoid harassment because they were of a different race, ethnic background, or lifestyle than the dominant group in the community. Sad as it is, hate crimes still exist, and people are hurt daily by the acts of discrimination perpetrated by other people.

The impacts of hate crimes range from small amounts of property damage to homicide. Victims of hate crimes generally have feelings of intense anger that they have been treated badly through no fault of their own. They have a growing fear that such a crime will happen to them again, so they spend great amounts of energy to avoid a possible recurrence. They may experience feelings of powerlessness and depression. Some victims experience great urges to retaliate. Once people have been victims of hate crimes, it is generally more difficult for them to trust other people.[11]

In recent years, many cities and counties have passed hate crime ordinances in an attempt to stem the tide of growing, vigilante-style violence. It remains to be seen whether these ordinances will help or not. However, one thing for certain is that the victims of hate crimes need people who will be neighbors to them.

Victims of Street Violence

Every major city in this country has problems of violence on its streets. These acts of violence range from drive-by shootings to youth-on-youth combat. The problems is classified by many as epidemic in its proportions. One has only to listen to the daily news to find evidence to support this classification. In our nation's capital, the Emergency Medical Services reported a 660 percent increase in shootings involving children aged 15 or younger in a 7-year period of 1985–92.

Human Immunodeficiency Virus (HIV) and Acquired Immune Deficiency Syndrome (AIDS)

It is difficult to believe that prior to the decade of the 1980s acquired immune deficiency syndrome and human immuno-deficiency virus were not a part of the language of the general public. Now AIDS has become a world health problem. By mid-1994 more than 400,000 cases of AIDS had been reported in the United States, an expected 1 million people had tested positive for the HIV virus, and approximately 250,000 people had died from AIDS. In the United States, AIDS is the fourth leading cause of death in women between 25 and 44 years of age. In children between 1 and 4 years of age, it is the seventh leading cause of death.

AIDS is one of the most feared diseases of the 1990s. With this fear comes much misunderstanding. People who want to help must learn the facts about how HIV is and is not trans-mitted. We must be aware that no population group is im-mune. We are all at risk. We must be willing to help because individuals with HIV or AIDS, their families, and caregivers needs neighbors, not critics.

Summary

This chapter has been dedicated to answering two questions. Who are the people living near us who need merciful acts from a good Samaritan neighbor? Who are the people today needing to be ministered to by others who are following the witness and ministry model of Jesus?

Six population groups have been discussed here to suggest answers to these two questions: people who live in poverty, individuals and families who are homeless, subgroups within the elderly population, persons who cannot read or write, individuals and groups who are victims of violence, and persons with HIV or AIDS. These six groups are representative of the population in most communities in the

United States. The list is not comprehensive. It does not include individuals who are physically or mentally challenged, those who are in prison, or those who are experiencing discrimination because of their race, ethnicity, nationality, religion, or gender. And there are more.

Each of these population groups challenges the church to take a fresh look at the needs outside the church walls and start a new ministry. While no one church can do it all, for a church to do nothing is unacceptable. Christ's response to human need is the example we must follow in witness and ministry.

Learning Activities

1. Take a windshield tour of the community around your church. What do you see? What feelings do you have?

2. Review the census data for your church community. Let this new acquaintance with the community form a new perspective for you. As you review, make notes about the human needs you see. Which ones might be something you, your group, or your church can address?

3. Review the information in this chapter about people who work for minimum wage. Go to the grocery store and see what kinds of meals you can plan for you and three children. Remember that you can spend only $1.16 per person per meal.

4. When you have decided on a particular meal that you can afford, invite three of your friends from church to come over and share this meal with you. Tell them that the purpose of this meal is to understand how it feels to be poor.

5. Volunteer to work for a day in a homeless shelter for families. Before you go think about what you expect to find. After the day is over, see if there are some things that were different from what you expected. Have your feelings about the homeless changed?

6. Make arrangements for your group to visit a congregate meal sight, and talk with the people while they are having

lunch. Or arrange for members of your group to accompany a volunteer who delivers meals to the homebound. Later, discuss with your group what you learned and felt from these experiences.

7. Talk to an adult child who is the primary caregiver for a parent who is frail. Ask this caregiver what he or she needs and what your group might be able to do to help.

8. Find out from experts in your community what percentage of the population cannot functionally read and write. Find out if there are people available who can train others to teach adult literacy. What did you learn about this population group?

9. Have someone from a local spouse abuse program speak to your group about what it is like to be victim of domestic violence.

10. Read your local newspaper to gather as much information as you can about the incidences of child abuse in your community. Have someone from a Baptist children's home program speak to your group on this subject. Be sure to focus on what the life situation is and on what you might do to be a neighbor to these children and their families.

11. Revise your list of needs discovered during the windshield tour. What did you add and why?

5

Starting New Ministries: Assessment and Ministry Selection

We have studied the way Christ responded to human need. We have given ourselves a reality check on turning stumbling blocks into stepping stones. We have increased our awareness of the people groups who need neighbors. The challenge to believers is to structure ways we can follow Christ's example. That is what this chapter is about.

The process of starting a new ministry must begin and continue with prayer. The Jesus model dictates this. As believers we are convinced that we need God's guidance in every venture of our lives. Starting a new ministry is no exception. We must pray for God's will to guide our efforts. Our prayers should include all the people who will be involved: those individuals, families, and communities who will be served in Jesus' name; those people who will be the servant helpers; those people who will be our partners in the helping network; those to whom the new ministry will be a witness simply because they see it happen or hear about it from those involved.

A new ministry can be started by any number of configurations of people in a local church. It can be initiated by one individual, an informal group, an organization such as Woman's Missionary Union, a missions development council or committee, or other groups. However, regardless of who starts a new ministry, there is a generic process which must guide the effort step by step. Following this program development process is the best way to insure that the ministry will enhance the lives of all people involved and be a healthy witness to the love and compassion of Jesus.

Assessments
The first step in developing new ministries is to determine available resources. While it may seem more appropriate to

begin by discovering the needs in your church's community, it is best to see first what resources you have. A realistic assessment of the resources available will help in several ways. First, it will encourage people by letting them know from the start that they will not be drawn into a project for which they are not prepared. Second, the resource assessment will help your group set realistic boundaries early in the process so you will not spend time analyzing needs which are beyond your means and abilities to meet. Third, it will help convince those who are likely to participate that the ministry goals can be accomplished.

People Resources

The first step in a resource assessment is to find out what kind of people power is available and how much of it is available. Since ministry and witness are people intense, it is essential that you have enough people with gifts to match the ministry and witness tasks you discover in the needs assessment, which comes later. As you go about assessing the people resources, remember that you are doing them a great favor. You are providing them with a chance to grow in Christ.

Ministry, if it follows the model Jesus displayed, has the potential to help everyone involved. Obviously, it will help those for whom the ministry is done. What is less obvious is that it often changes the lives of those servant helpers who carry it out. The doers reach a more mature level of Christian discipleship. We see this happen over and over in partnership missions. People testify participation in a ministry is a life-changing experience. This is true for new Christians as well as mature ones. It is especially true for those Christians, as well as churches, that I characterize as adolescents in their Christian development.

Adolescents work through certain developmental tasks through which youth have to work through to move on to adulthood. They have to come to terms with who they are and what is important to them. As they work their way through these tasks, certain characteristics seem to stand out. The same developmental processes take place in Christian growth and discipleship. This maturing process is illustrated in the interpretation of the parable of the sower in Luke 8:11–15.

Those of us who are around teenagers know that they are concerned with what is fair. For example, if someone else gets to do something their parents will not let them do, they do not think their parents are fair. If someone else has designer jeans and they do not, this is not fair. Their whole world seems to revolve around what is in it for them and making sure they get their share. They are self-interested and self-centered.

Teenagers are also fickle in their relationships and moods. Today's best friend can become tomorrow's worst enemy. Relationships among peers change often, twisting and turning with each new day. Teens are sorting out characteristics they like and dislike in people. Often these mood swings reflect physiological and social changes taking place. Because teenagers act one way one day does not mean they will act the same way the next time you meet them in similar situations. They are not consistent.

Teenagers are sensitive and reactive. They react according to the way the world is treating them. Again, they are their main agenda. They have not learned how to see themselves as a part of a world or a family. The center around which they make their life decisions is self, with little regard for how the rest of the group is impacted. They lack basic commitment to empathize with those outside their peer group.

Adolescents work very hard to fit in; they want to look and be like their peers. They want to be with people who look like they look, act like they act, and value what is important to them as individuals. This is natural for their chronological age. They are not interested in making individual stands on ethical issues. The fact that their peer group is so important to them makes them enormously susceptible to pressure from that group. People who are different are not valued as a part of the *in* group.

We have learned to accept these characteristics and behaviors in teenagers. We understand that this is a natural part of growing up. However, when these characteristics and behaviors persist in people who have reached their adult years, we find them unacceptable ways of being and doing. Adults who act like teenagers are seen as insensitive and irresponsible.

I describe adolescent churches or Christians as those who have not yet established who they are or what is essentially important to them. They like to worship with people who look like they look, act like they act, and dress like they dress. Their understanding of who God is does not serve them well when life is not fair. They approach faith and worship as spectators who receive rather than as servants who give and are forgiven.

They are fickle in their relationships and are easily led by charismatic leaders without thinking through what the leader is saying or where the leader is going. These churches and individuals see themselves as the focus and tend to seek others to care for their hurts rather than taking on the caring role themselves.

Time and time again, I have witnessed churches and people who take the risk and grow into adulthood. This new growth in discipleship most often comes when people and churches get involved in ministries to others. I do not know all the dynamics. I do know that helping other people seems to call forth in us a refocusing of our energies on caring for others more than we care for ourselves. This seems to trigger new growth in Christians. Involvement in missions and ministries also seems to help us better understand the realities of pain and suffering. We become more aware, more compassionate, and more caring. All of this helps us mature in our faith.

The point to be made here is that as you assess the people resources available, remember that everyone is a potential servant helper. The assessment of people resources may require helping people discover that they indeed are resources. For example, individuals may need help identifying their spiritual gifts. They may feel they do not have anything to offer in the way of helping others. My ministry experience has taught me that while most Christians are aware of the biblical material on gifts in 1 Corinthians 12, Romans 12, Ephesians 4, 1 Peter 4, and Hebrews 2, they are often not able to identify their own gifts. They may need to learn these biblical teachings:

1. God has given every Christian at least one gift;
2. Each Christian is responsible for helping other Christians identify and affirm their gifts;
3. All Christians are responsible for developing and using their gifts to carry out the ministries of the church for the common good;
4. Since no one gift is greater than another, they provide no basis for pride; and
5. Each gift is essential in order for the whole body to work together to do God's will.

You may need to help members of your group discover their spiritual gifts.

On a less formal basis, you may simply ask members of your group to list the things they enjoy and are interested in doing, and those things which energize them. Another way to help people identify gifts is to ask them what sufferings of others touch their hearts. Gifts often give us keen insight and deep empathy for hurting humanity. People whose hearts are broken for others who suffer from a particular life situation likely have a gift to help those they see in that situation. It just seems to be the way God works with His followers.

When gifts are identified and acknowledged, some record should be made of the discoveries. This record can be a simple sheet in a notebook on which is recorded basic information about individuals and their gifts. In a more elaborate form, this can be a database kept on a computer. In some churches, databases which contain a section on ministry interests and gifts may already be available. In such cases, you need to secure copies of the data and update them. This information will become a vital part of your resource assessment.

A discovery of your group's gifts is the first step. Next, determine how much time these people have to devote to starting a new ministry in the church community. If there are particular circumstances which limit the amount of time people have, this needs to be known. If work schedules make it impossible for people to be involved during certain hours, this needs to be noted.

While there are certainly legitimate demands on the time people have to do ministry, most people find time to do what is important and enjoyable to them. As you go about gathering this information, do not hesitate to ask busy people.

Financial Resources

Many ministries do not require that you invest large sums of personal or church money in order to participate in them. Often, such ministries are funded through donations, grants from private and religious foundations, and/or fees charged for services rendered. Implement research to determine if money is available, and if so, how much. Learning how your church currently funds its ministries in the community is a place to start. What funds are available from within the church? What are the church's policies and standards for securing financial support for its ministries? Are monies that might fund the project available from private and religious foundations? The librarian at the local public library or university will be able to help you find answers to these questions. What if the ministry you later decide to start needs to charge fees? Is this possible under the policies of your church or group? All of these are questions which must be answered in the resource assessment.

In-Kind Resources
In-kind resources are those donated items not measured in dollars and cents. Such resources may include the use of a room, furniture, telephone, and so forth. What in-kind resources are available to you? Is there space at your church that can be used on a regular basis for a new ministry among people who live in the community even though they are not currently members of your church? Is there another place in the community more appropriate for a particular ministry than space at the church? For example, is there a community center in a housing project that might be able to provide meeting space? Does your church own a van you can use to transport people? If not, are there members of your ministry groups willing to transport people in their own vehicles? Does the local Red Cross or local housing authority provide transportation for its clients?

Think of all the possible in-kind resources that might be available to you. If you live in a rural area, what in-kind services might be available through the Extension Department of the local office of the Department of Agriculture? What resources may be available through service clubs and local schools?

These ideas are not comprehensive; they are suggestions for discovering what resources are available for starting a new ministry. You will know other resources in your community. Conduct a resource inventory and keep a record of all you find.

Needs Assessment
Once you have a good idea of what resources are available, you are ready to turn to the needs assessment. The new ministry start should address a real need. Often our perceptions of the community's needs are incorrect. At first glance, we may not be able to identify what the potential clients perceive as the real or most pressing needs. The generally acceptable ways to carry out a needs assessment are US Census Data review, key informant interviews, community resident interviews, and surveys of

members of your church's congregation. While all of these may not need to be done, at least two should be done to give the findings a check and balance.

Review of Census Data

Census data is available at federal depository libraries. These may be local public libraries or college/university libraries. Your local librarian can tell you the locations of the federal depository libraries near you. Census data is also available on Internet which can be accessed through various commercial gateways. If none of these services are available, you can write the Census Bureau in Washington, DC, or contact your United States congressional representatives. Either the Census Bureau or your senators or representatives in Congress will make available to you the data for the particular community in which your church is located. Often your Baptist state convention headquarters will have the census data and be glad to share it with you.

From the census data, you can learn the median age and number of people in each census track in a given geographical area. You can find the educational level, income level, and minority demographics of the community. The data will also indicate the types of housing available as well as how many people live in each unit and whether or not the housing is substandard. The number of mother-only families and two parent families will be listed as well. A review of the demographics will provide a good overview of all the people characteristics of any particular area. After reviewing this data, it is a good idea to go on a windshield tour of your community. Drive through the area and determine if what you see matches the census data. Make a note of questions that come to mind as you drive through the community. Later, you can ask experts to respond to these questions.

Key Informant Interviews

A key informant is a person who lives, works, or interacts within a community. Another way to determine the needs of a community is to initiate conversation with these community experts to find out what needs they encounter each day. Talk to public officials who serve the neighborhood. Police officers, firefighters, or representatives of the offices of the mayor, county judge, or city manager are all good resources. Meet with school principals and teachers. Interview social workers, staff members of local mental health programs, and other social service agency personnel. Talk to staff members in other churches in the neighborhood to get their assessments of the needs. Interview medical personnel such as emergency medical service workers and public health officials. Interview business and civic leaders and realtors.

Think of other people who work in or provide services to the community. Ask them what the needs are. Interview juvenile justice workers, judges, and other court personnel. In some instances you may want to invite people such as public health nurses, social workers, or police officers to come and speak to your groups about their perceptions of the needs of people in your church community.

Interaction with key informants affords you firsthand information about the needs of your community. Identify a list of key informants in your community and divide the list among your members. After the interviews, compile a list of the needs cited. Check this list against the findings from the census data. Now you should have a beginning list of real needs that exist in your community.

Resident Interviews

A third way to do a needs assessment is to interview people who live in the area, asking them what they think the neighborhood problems are. Since you probably cannot interview everyone, randomly select streets in the neighborhood. Then try to interview people who live in every fifth or every tenth house on the street.

Have members of your group form survey teams. Write out a standard introduction for each team to use and prepare an identification badge for each member of the team. Discuss general safety precautions with each team. No one is to go alone. It is safer to talk with people without entering their houses. Prepare a set of questions for each interview team to ask of the people they can find at home. Have one team member ask the questions while the other member writes down the responses. Be sure to ask permission from the person being interviewed to write down their responses.

These interview questions should focus on two areas: What do you think is good about your neighborhood? What do you think people in your neighborhood need to make their lives better? It is better to ask the "what is good about your community" questions first. If you ask the "what does your community need" questions first, the people may assume that needs are all you think they have.

Another approach would be to prepare a list of issues raised by the key informant or the census data. Ask the neighborhood residents to rank the listed items from the most urgent to least urgent. At the end of the ranking, ask them if they would like to add anything else to the list.

When the interviews are done, compile one master list from all the resident interviews, ranking the needs in order of importance from most urgent to least urgent. Double check the list against all the other data you have. Are your findings consistent with what you learned previously? Are there needs not mentioned before? Are there inconsistencies in the rankings of the residents and other sources of information you have gathered? At this point there should be a few needs which have been evident in all of your sources. These are the needs to which you want to pay particular attention.

Congregational Surveys

Another way to assess needs is to do a paper and pencil survey of the youth and adult members of your church congregation. Ask them to list in priority order what they consider to be the three greatest needs of your community or the area you identify as your ministry neighborhood. Compile a list of all the responses. Give a value of three to all the first choices, a value of two to all the second choices, and a value of one to all the third choices. Then add the values for each item and divide by the number of people who listed that particular item. The scores will allow you to rank the needs as seen through the eyes of the congregation.

Another way to conduct a congregational survey is to secure copies of the *Church/Community Needs Survey Guide (301-28F)* from the North American Mission Board, SBC. This paper and pencil survey can be completed by any configuration of people who are in the older youth or adult age groups. Once the survey is administered, the results can be compiled and prioritized based on the number of people who identified an item as an area of need. As you carry out the needs assessment, remember that every community has needs and resources.

It is important to involve as many people as possible in gathering data. Every individual who participates will learn something new about the needs of the community. Even those who may have been skeptical in the beginning often will be influenced by hearing people tell their stories.

Matching Needs and Resources

At this point in the process, you may feel you are overwhelmed with data. This is a good sign that you have done your work well. Now it is time to take the resource assessment results and the needs assessment findings and compare them to see what resources and needs match. For example, suppose you discover there is a great need in your community to help children and youth stay in school. You also find that a number of people in your resource pool are gifted teachers who like to work with youth or people who would like to tutor or be a mentor to youth. You have a match, and where you find such matches, you identify potential new ministry starts.

Make a list of all the potential matches that emerge from your assessments of needs and resources. At this point you already know a good deal about both. However, you should now focus on what kind of interventions will be most effective and efficient. Take each of the matches and think your way through three questions: How will the ministry be structured or configured? How long will the ministry remain in effect? What will the objectives of the ministry be? An in-depth discussion of the factors in this three-way matrix will be presented next to guide your thinking.

Different Ministry Configurations

Most ministries fall in one of four configurations. Ministries can be designed to network with existing service providers, to link with other service providers, to host a program, or to start an independent program of ministry. You will need to think about which of these configurations will best serve as a context for meeting the matched needs and resources you have identified.

Networking with Existing Service Providers

In most communities and most situations of need there are helping people, agencies, and institutions already present and working to meet the need. Schools, hospitals, social service agencies, other faith groups, other churches, and public services are a few examples of these. One way to configure your new ministry is to network with these existing groups.

If several people in your resource pool are interested in helping victims of spouse abuse, you may want to see if there is a local center for women and families or a local spouse abuse shelter already in operation. If there is, check with the volunteer coordinator at the shelter and offer help. The shelter and its supporting agencies will provide the special training church members need in order to work with people who have been abused. Perhaps you have several people who want to help with feeding programs for the frail elderly. You may want to get them involved in Meals on Wheels programs or encourage them to volunteer as food servers at a local congregate nutrition program meal site. The list of networking possibilities is endless.

One benefit of this configuration is that you do not duplicate services. In addition, established agencies and services generally will have highly developed volunteer training programs for the people from your resource pool. Another benefit is that the people who are serving from your church will have opportunities to meet other helping people with like interest in and commitment to the clients. Christians will find many opportunities to be salt, light, and leaven as they mix and mingle with people outside their usual traffic patterns.

In this configuration, the question always raised is whether or not this might limit Christians' verbal witness of their personal faith in Jesus Christ. While there may be such limitations placed on verbal witnessing in some instances, I have found that the helping witness makes a profound impact in those settings. You will also find many Christians already on the staffs of these agencies and programs. They need your support and encouragement. Another thing to remember is that many of the clients you will meet are already Christians.

The rule of thumb is that you can talk to clients about anything they bring up. When you introduce yourself and tell them that you are from such and such a church, the conversations about faith generally emerge naturally. If you follow the ministry model of Jesus as described in Luke, people will see that you care. When they experience your mercy and compassion, you will have ample opportunities to witness. God will see to that.

Linking with Other Service Providers

Linking with other service providers is different from networking. In the networking configuration, people from the church actually go into the setting and become part of the volunteer staff of that agency or program. In the linking configuration, as used here, a new program is started and operated by the church but is linked in some way with another service provider.

For example, you may want to start an after-school tutoring program. The participants would meet at the church and your group would be totally responsible for its operation. However, you would be linked to the local elementary school who would refer children to your program and guide those adults who tutor by providing a description of the learning needs of the youth. In addition, the principal or teachers in the school may be able to provide copies of textbooks and learning assignments for the children in the program to follow.

You might have a group of women in your resource pool who want to help teen mothers learn how to care for their infant children. You secure a room at a community center in a public housing development because your needs assessment says that a number of teen mothers live in or near the development. Your group is responsible for the entire program. Your link with the housing authority is the use of its space and the consultation of one of its social workers.

These are examples of what I call "linking with other service providers" programs. As in the networking programs, the benefit of a linking program is that you become a part of the larger helping community. In addition, you gain access to resources of space, expertise, and guidance that you would not otherwise have. In this configuration you gain more control over what you are able to do and more freedom for verbal witness. The only constraints that you have are the general policies regarding space usage and staff consultation set by the host agency.

Hosting a Program

Another configuration that some churches and individuals find possible is providing space, expertise, or resources for a ministry while inviting a program group to come in and carry out the program activity. For example, the church might provide space for another group to come in and operate a day-care center for the community. It may be obvious that the church does not have the expertise or people resources to operate a child development center. However, the church does have space that is not being used during the week and which meets all the public health and safety codes. This space, janitorial services, and utilities can be made available to a nearby community center which has the resources to operate the child development center but does not have space for it. Another example is that many churches have kitchens and dining rooms that could be made available as congregate meal sites for older adults. A local food service for older adults may provide the food, servers, and clean-up crew. The church provides space for food preparation and consumption.

The advantage of hosting a ministry is that small churches can make significant contributions to the meeting of a community need while not overextending their resources. Hosting a ministry also gives the church a chance to demonstrate to the community that it is a caring church wanting to help in any way it can. The major limitation of this model is that often it does not give the servant helpers from the church an opportunity for much face-to-face contact with the people who come for the service.

Starting an Independent Program
In some situations, the need and resource matches indicate it is best to start a program for which you are totally responsible and that does not officially network or link with any other group. Some churches are large enough to start their own mission, ministry center, neighborhood food pantry, or other program. However, this is the exception rather than the rule.

The major advantage of an independent program is that the church is fully responsible for what goes on and more people from the church can be involved. The major concern is making sure the program is not duplicating what someone else is doing. You must carefully consider which of these configurations will best serve your ministry efforts.

Ministry Classifications According to Duration
The effectiveness and efficiency of ministries are often limited because no one takes time at the onset to decide how long the program of ministry should remain in effect. Sometimes needs which demand a long-term commitment are addressed with short-term interventions. Then the question is asked, why did

we not make a difference? Sometimes needs which could have been met with short-term interventions have been allowed to go on and on until everyone gets tired and people stop coming. Also, there are needs that can be addressed in a medium length of time.

For example, if you decide to help women in mother-only families become self-sufficient and escape from poverty, you should know from the start that this will take three to four years or longer. If you have people in your resource pool who want to teach English as a second language to internationals, this may take one to two years. After-school tutoring programs may run only nine months to coincide with the school year. If you decide to provide a recognition banquet for the youth at the local Baptist center who complete high school, you would need only a few months to organize, implement, and complete the project.

It is extremely important to make a decision about time before you start. If you select the right length of time for your ministry, you will enhance your potential for success. People are more willing to sign on if they know when the task will end. If you determine the duration of a project before you begin, both the servant helpers and the client group will know when the ministry is going to conclude.

Ministries conducted for a month or less are generally referred to as short-term; medium-term ministries last two months to one year, and long-term projects take up more than a year's time. Even if you are designing a program that is going to last more than a year, it is wise to renew your commitment at least once a year and to refocus your intervention goals based on what you have learned during the course of the past 12 months. Things do change!

Selecting Change Objectives

Not only do you need to select a configuration and duration for your match of resources and needs; you also need to decide which change objectives seem to be indicated by the nature of the needs and resources. There are numerous lists of change objectives available in books on helping. However, for our purposes here, I have selected the list composed by Edwin J. Thomas because it is representative of most other lists. His list includes remediation, enhancement, competence, education, prevention, advocacy, resource provision, and social control.[12]

Remediation

Remediation is helping people to resolve a problem that is causing them to be unable to function as they usually do. Many circumstances call for such ministries. Examples include a father/husband who loses his job, a mother and daughter who can no longer communicate effectively with each other, or a young boy who suffers physical disabilities as a result of a boating accident.

The need for remediation exists when something has happened to people or their families, or in their social environment, which causes them to have a problem. If the problem can be resolved, these people can go back to functioning the way they did before. However, if the problems are not addressed, the debilitating effects will become more and more severe, leading to a more troublesome life situation. Your goal here is not to move them past where they were before the problem arose, but to help them catch up with where they would have been had the problem not occurred.

Enhancement

Enhancement objectives in helping are designed to take people who are already functioning at a satisfactory level and help them reach new levels of functioning to help themselves and their families. Programs such as cultural enrichment, divorce recovery workshops, art appreciation, marriage enrichment, nutrition improvement, and adventure clubs are a few examples of enhancement ministries. In this kind of helping your goals are to encourage people who are making it to reach greater levels of satisfaction.

Competence

Competence objectives are intended to help people solve problems that currently exist and also to teach skills that will help them solve similar problems which may arise in the future. For example, suppose a single parent is employed and earns enough money to support herself and her young son. However, she does not know how to manage the money and finds that by the third week in each month her financial resources have been depleted. If you are able to help her become competent in managing her money now, this same competence will serve her in future financial crises.

A parent who is unable to handle his or her frustration with a hard-to-manage child is another example of someone who might benefit from a competence ministry. Sometimes the parental frustration level reaches such heights that parents are afraid they will abuse their child. If you teach the parent how to better handle the child and how to cool off and deal with his or her own frustrations, she or he may be able to use some of the cooling off techniques at work when frustrations on the job become almost unbearable.

Education

Education is a significant part of helping. Education objectives are geared to helping people have the correct information they need to deal with problems of living. In almost every living situation, more information is helpful. Some examples of this kind of helping might be teaching people what to expect if a member of their family has Alzheimer's disease; if they have just been diagnosed as having diabetes; if they have learned that their teenage daughter is taking illegal drugs; or if a family member is mentally retarded. In each of these instances, managing the situation requires that the caregivers know what to expect in the way of adverse effects, the typical course of the illness or problem, and the best plans of care. Information about how to cope with the situation and how families can support the person involved is essential. Dealing with a teenager on drugs is difficult even when parents have all the available information about drug abuse. Without the information, coping is impossible.

Prevention

Prevention is a change objective which seeks to keep problems from developing. For example, if children are helped to learn to read and are mentored early in their school experiences, the chances are increased that they will stay in school and graduate. Edwin Thomas says that if you can teach children skills in "conflict resolution, communication, and decision making" in early life, you will be contributing to the prevention of violence later in their lives. There are any number of homeless prevention programs being implemented in cities all over this country. Helping people get employment or helping them deal with financial difficulties early on and learn to manage their affairs in more efficient ways will prevent a lot of families from becoming homeless.

Advocacy

Advocacy is standing up for individuals or groups whose rights are being violated or who are the targets of discrimination. It also means working to see that the interests of vulnerable or powerless groups are respected and responded to by the power brokers.

For example, a public utility company is cutting off the water or electricity at homes when people fall behind in their payments. Church groups can get together and negotiate with these utility companies for certain time allowances before the cut-offs occur, especially if temperatures fall below or rise above certain levels. You may find that one of the ways you can minister is to work with aldermen or county commissioners to see that police drive drug dealers out of neighborhoods. Perhaps you find that your community does not have a spouse abuse shelter and you work with local officials to establish one. These are advocacy efforts . . . using the power you have on behalf of those who have less power.

It is interesting to note that one of the functions of the Holy Spirit is being an advocate for the believer, walking alongside of and enabling and empowering him. These are the same functions which advocates carry out today.

One example of an advocacy program found in many communities is a review panel for foster children. In these review panels, advocates work under the supervision of state human resources cabinets. They read files and make sure that foster children are not shuttled between foster homes and forgotten.

The aim of advocacy is to work to change a system that may be abusive in and of itself. In addition, it is to empower the powerless and to work on behalf of those who are too beaten down to stand up for themselves.

A story has circulated in the helping world for a number of years, although its originator is long forgotten. The story involves a man who decided he wanted to go fishing. He got his pole and bait and set out for the river. Once at the river, he baited his hook and sat down to enjoy an afternoon of fishing. Not long after he put his bait in the water a man came thrashing down the river shouting, "Help me! Help me! I'm drowning!"

The man put down his pole and rescued the drowning man. Once this was done, he started fishing again. After a little while, another man floated down the river yelling, "Help me! Help me! I'm drowning!" The man put down his pole and rescued the second man. Within the next hour a dozen people floated down the river screaming to be rescued. The fisherman saved each individual as he or she floated by him.

Finally the fisherman had to make a choice. He could give up trying to fish and rescue each person who floated by calling out for help, or he could walk up the river to see who was throwing these people into the water. Advocacy is a way of going upstream and helping to change a situation that causes people to be hurting. In religious life, we refer to this as prophetic or social justice ministry.

Resource Provision

Resource provision is helping by seeing that people have the resources they need to live and care for themselves and their families. Clothing ministries, feeding stations, medical clinics, shelter, money to pay utilities, school supplies, college scholarships, clothing appropriate for job interviews, and uniforms and steel-toed shoes for work are all examples of resources provided by different ministries of local churches.

The aim of resource provision is to help people who cannot solve a problem because they do not have the material resources to get started. A woman has a job but there is no public transportation and she has no car. A man cannot go to work unless he can provide his own tools. Children need glasses to see the chalkboard in school. An older adult must have dentures in order to work at a local fast food restaurant. In cases of rape, the police confiscate the victim's underclothes as evidence, and at one of the most vulnerable times in her life, she finds she has no undergarment to wear home. The list of needed resources is endless.

Social Control

Social control kinds of helping are usually carried out by public agencies authorized by legislation to be agents of social control. This kind of helping is designed to either protect a vulnerable population or protect the general population from people who commit crimes. Children, elderly people, and persons who need special protection such as the mentally impaired are examples of the vulnerable groups for which the rest of the population has special responsibility. Legal offenders, on the other hand, are those from whom society needs protection.

Ministries in this category are usually residential in nature. Children's homes and all levels of residential services to older adults fall into the first category. Prisons and other correctional institutions fall in the second category.

Most of the ministries with social control objectives will of necessity involve networking with other service providers. These providers are licensed by the state to provide this care or are operated by the state or federal departments of human services or corrections under mandates from state and federal legislative bodies.

These eight helping or change objectives have been presented as separate entities, but it should be noted that some programs may have several of these objectives as their goals. For example, Woman's Missionary Union has designed a ministry to help women on public assistance and welfare who want to become self-sustaining. Through a program of mentoring, training, job seeking, and support, members of WMU will be the servant helpers. In this instance there are several change objectives. Competence, education, prevention, advocacy, and resource provision are all part of the helping interventions of this program.

Summary

The aim of this chapter has been to guide you to select a ministry project or program that will meet a real need. This ministry is to be a program or project for which resources are available. It is time now to review all the data and select one or more ministries that you will begin or in which you will serve. Here is a review of the checklist of incremental decisions that should guide your choices. Remember, this entire process should be a focus of prayer by your group!

Step 1. Review the resource assessment results.

Step 2. Rethink the needs assessment findings.

Step 3. Make a list of all the possible matches.

Step 4. Put this list of matches in order of priority based on the strength of the match.

Step 5. Take the top three matches and think about them in light of three questions.
    A. What configuration will best serve to move you to your goal?
        1. Networking with existing service providers
        2. Linking with existing service providers
        3. Hosting a program
        4. Starting an independent ministry
    B. How long will the ministry need to last?
        1. Long-term
        2. Medium-term
        3. Short-term
    C. What change objectives will best help the people to whom we minister?
        1. Remediation
        2. Enhancement
        3. Competence
        4. Education
        5. Prevention
        6. Advocacy
        7. Resource Provision
        8. Social Control

Step 6. In light of step 5, rethink the priorities of the top three matches.

Step 7. Select the top priority and write out goal(s).

Your goals should include what you plan to accomplish, the group with whom you will conduct the ministry, the configuration of the ministry, and the change objectives you select. One way of writing goals is to put them in the form of a program hypothesis. Peter Kettner, Robert Moroney, and Lawrence Martin provide such an example in the case of a program to help women in mother-only families become economically self-sufficient.

"If women can acquire marketable job skills, and if they are assisted in finding employment in the primary labor market, and if they are relieved of their child-care responsibilities by the provision of quality child care, then they are likely to complete their training, secure and retain employment, and raise their standard of living to reasonable levels.

Furthermore, in some instances, if child support is provided to the mother, that mother will have more options open to her. Not only would she be in a position to increase her family income, but she could also choose between part- and full-time work outside the home and even to return to school as a first step in establishing a career."[13]

Learning Activities

1. Make a list of the kinds of resources needed in ministries. Begin to jot down items that come to mind as you think of the resources you or your group have. Keep this running list. You will be able to use it later.

2. Read and study all the Scriptures that relate to spiritual gifts. Begin to identify your gifts and help others in your group identify their gifts. Encourage your group to have a workshop on spiritual gifts.

3. Visit your local library and read as much as you can on how to carry out a needs assessment. If you have a United Way agency or other umbrella helping organization near you, ask them for copies of any recent needs assessments they may have on your community. Discuss these findings with your group or church committee. Begin to get people talking about the needs in your community.

4. Make a list of key informants who can help you discover the needs in the community around your church. Follow the suggestions in the chapter, but add others as well.

5. Write to the North American Mission Board and order a copy of the church community needs survey. Decide if it is something you may want to use later in your church.

6. Review the different ministry configurations discussed in this chapter. Which of these fits within the policies and goals of your church's missions outreach strategy?

7. Think about change objectives as described in this chapter. Which of these seems to best fit the competencies of the members of your group? Which of these can you do and still stay within the limits of your resources? Which of these, if any, are not appropriate for your group to undertake? Why?

6

Starting New Ministries: Design, Implementation, and Evaluation

Once the needs and resources have been assessed and the program goals written, the next steps are program design, implementation, and evaluation. These steps form the second half of the process of starting new ministries. Remember that at each stage of this process, you need to pray for God's leadership, blessing, and guidance. Also keep in mind that you do need to follow the ministering model of Jesus outlined in Chapter 1.

Program Design

Program design, in its simplest form, is the choice of arrangements and actions which will best meet the ministry goals. For example, suppose your needs assessment identified a group of women living in your city or town who came to the United States from a non-English speaking country. Their husbands were transferred to the United States to manage a recently-opened automobile manufacturing plant. These women want to learn English as a second language (ESL) so they will be able to function in the culture and overcome the isolation they have felt since arriving here.

In your resource assessment you found several people in your group who have been interested in teaching English as a second language since they were trained to do so at a literacy workshop sponsored by your local association last year. Also, your resource inventory identified two teachers in a local high school who expressed an interest in volunteering to teach ESL classes. This is the match your group selected to guide the start of a new ministry. Your new ministry goal is to engage these resource people to teach international women to read, write, and converse in English.

97

Your program hypothesis is that if women for whom English is a second language can acquire skills in reading, writing, and speaking English, they will feel less social isolation and be more competent in essential interactions with individuals, groups, and institutions in their community. Examples of such interactions may be with doctors, schoolteachers, and clerks in grocery stores.

However, before a specific plan of action for implementing the program is developed, several important preliminary issues need to be addressed or revisited. These issues are leadership group, program configurations, change objectives, measures of success, approvals and sponsorships, risk management, and procedures for handling money.

Leadership Group

While some ministries may be started by an individual, most are initiated by a leadership group. This may be a steering committee, representatives from the sponsoring group, or some other organization. (It was assumed in the previous chapter the group that conducts the need and resource assessments and selects the target goals is also the group that initiates the ministry.) This leadership group becomes even more important in the design, implementation, and evaluation phases of starting a new ministry.

This group will guide efforts to secure sponsorship, recruit servant leaders, engage clients, format the program, and monitor the implementation and evaluation. It is essential that the leadership group is committed to seeing each of these tasks through to a satisfactory and timely conclusion. Without such a leadership group, the program initiative will likely flounder and never be fully implemented.

Variations in Program Configuration

Leadership groups should select a program configuration that will best facilitate the goals of their planned ministry. There are several possible program configurations, including networking with existing service providers, linking with existing service providers, hosting programs, and starting independent ministries, and each calls for a different kind of program design.

For example, if you are networking with existing service providers, the program design will involve connecting the people in your church who want to volunteer with the service provider's director of volunteer services. In addition to this connection, some means of providing resources, support, and recognition for these church members may be necessary. However, beyond this there is little else that needs to be done. If other issues arise, they can be dealt with on an as-needed basis. If you select the configuration of linking with another resource provider, then the format of your program and the ways you engage clients will be different. For example, if you link with a local elementary school to start a tutoring program, the school counselors and teachers would provide the lesson plans and refer students to your program. Remember that your program design must fit the configuration you choose because that configuration will best meet your goals.

Change Objectives
Review your choice of change objectives. The eight change objectives listed in the previous chapter included remediation, enhancement, competence, education, prevention, advocacy, resource provision, and social control. The ones your group selects will be determined by your goals. This selection will shape a significant part of the program design. If you decide on remediation you will need to go in one direction. However, if you choose resource provision, you might need to design a different kind of program. Remember that all the choices presented in Chapter 4 bring different shapes to the program design, implementation, and evaluation phases.

Measures of Success
Evaluation will be discussed indepth later in this chapter. However, several things need to be put in place now to make evaluation possible later. First, evaluation involves accountability for or stewardship of resources. Secondly, it requires some measure of effectiveness. Did we do what we set out to do? Did we utilize our resources of people, money, and in-kind items to produce the most effective and efficient outcomes possible?

At the end of the program, in order to determine if it did what we set out to do, some measures of success have to be determined at the onset. To do this, the goals must be translated into measurable objectives. For example, in the goal of teaching English as a second language to international women, the objectives might be that by the end of the program year:

1. ten women will have learned to read the daily newspaper;
2. eight women will have learned how to write a letter in English to a company to stop a magazine subscription;
3. twelve women will have learned how to call 911 and, using only English, report a family emergency; and
4. twelve women will know about the workers' Christian faith experiences with Jesus.

Each of these objectives, if well written, should include a measure of success. One way to determine if your objectives are sound is to see if the objectives make measuring success possible. If you review an objective and are still confused as to how to determine whether or not you met the objective, then it is not well written.

To determine whether or not the resources were used to the best advantage, you will need data regarding resource use as well as standards of success for use of resources. For example, we have used our resources well if at the end of the program:

1. the servant helpers report that the experience has been one that helped them to grow in discipleship;
2. the servant helpers report that they are more sensitive to people who need help or have had to rethink some prejudice they may have harbored;
3. all funds have been accounted for and all bills paid while staying within the approved budget;
4. people who provided in-kind resources of space are satisfied with how the program workers cared for this space.

With these kinds of specific measures of success, it will be possible to gather the data you will need during and at the end of the implementation to evaluate the effectiveness and efficiency of the program

Getting Appropriate Approvals and Sponsorships

Most new ministry starts will need to be sponsored by a missions organization, group, or church. These sponsorships involve getting groups to take ownership of the ministry, set its policies, and contribute to its pool of resources. In these instances, there will be approval policies and procedures for securing this ownership of and commitment to ministry initiatives.

It is a mistake to start a new ministry and then seek to get sponsorship from a group that did not have any say in the starting of the ministry and has made no official commitment to it. It is not uncommon, when working with church groups, to hear about problems caused when one or two people go out and start a ministry and expect an organization or church to assume responsibility for staffing and paying for it.

If a church's missions committee refuses to sponsor a ministry for good reason, the promoters are often upset. One of the most likely outcomes is that these promoters will try to get other church members to designate their offerings to pay for the ministry. Since these designations take money out of the regular budget of the church, other church members may resent this kind of action. Before long, hostilities and fractures grow and more harm than good is done.

A better way is to bring everyone who will likely be involved on board as early as possible. Think of who needs to approve your program goals and whose help, if available, will be beneficial. Meet with these individuals and groups and try to secure the needed approval and support by making them allies of your effort. If you cannot get approval, see what you need to revise in order to try again. Most likely you will get approval to proceed. However, in the event you cannot get approval from the first group, think about other groups within the structure of your church that have within their assigned responsibilities the starting of new ministries. Present your ideas to them.

Risk Management

Before starting a ministry, attention must be given to risk management. What liabilities may be involved for whom? There may be significant risk in some programs and much less risk in others.

For example, if you are planning to open a free medical clinic for people in a rural area who have no access to medical care, the liabilities will be many and must be covered by insurance. On the other hand, if three women from your Women on Mission group are going to volunteer to serve meals at a nutrition site, the liabilities may be few. Transportation or escort services do involve liabilities. Are people going to use their private automobiles to transport people to and from the program? If so, how much liability insurance do they have and does your group need to purchase additional insurance? Are any of these liabilities covered by an insurance policy which your church already carries? All of these questions must be addressed by people who have expertise in matters of insurance and law. Perhaps there is an attorney among your members who would provide pro bono legal services. If you need liability insurance, purchase it.

Safety factors must be carefully reviewed. Do the facilities you plan to use meet fire and safety codes? Will stairs be used? If so, do they have handrailings? Are these facilities accessible to physically challenged people? If people who have hearing impairment are to be involved, are there fire alarm systems which will warn them? Will someone who has access to a telephone be present in the building at all times? Are evacuation plans made and available to occupants, especially small children or elderly people who are frail? Are there well-lighted parking spaces near the building? These are generic questions of health and safety. You may need to add other questions which are unique to your locality. For example, if your facility is located near chemical plants, you may want to find out what to do if there is a toxic spill.

Handling Money

In the event money is collected for any reason, whether for fees, dues, or purchase of supplies, make sure you have policies about who will be responsible for collecting, counting, keeping books, depositing money, and writing checks. At every step, from collecting to disbursing the money, at least two people should be present. They should count the money together and make out the deposit slips. They should both sign all the checks. This measure is a protection for the persons involved, and it reflects good money management practices. If a sizable amount of money will be collected, consider having the treasurer of the church or sponsoring organization set up an account and issue checks.

Recordkeeping and Reporting

In conducting record keeping and reporting, you must determine who needs to have what information and in what form they should receive it. Perhaps the sponsoring group will want monthly attendance figures and financial reports. The facilitator of your group may want to know how many servant helpers are involved and how much time, in clock hours, these people invested in the ministry. In your particular situation, there may be other entities to whom you need to report. Find out who they are and what they need to know.

Records need to be kept to provide the information for these reports. Do not waste time in keeping records which you will not use. However, be very diligent and accurate in keeping those that you do need. Be sure to assign this responsibility to someone who will be on site.

Design and Implementation

Formatting the Program Design

Now, let's consider the international women mentioned earlier in this chapter and the goal of helping them learn English as a second language. We will use the configuration of starting a new, independent ministry which will last one year with the change objectives of remediation and advocacy. The next step is to format the program.

You have the goal clearly in mind and you have the approval process underway. Now you can begin the formatting of your program. Formatting refers to the ideal image of what the program will look like and how it will operate if everything works in an ideal way.

Using the illustration of teaching international women English as a second language, dream on paper what the format of the program might be. Some questions to guide this imaging are stated here. What is your projected date for starting the program? What is the projected date for ending the program? Will everyone be available by that time? Where will you meet? How often will you meet? What day and time will you meet? What will you do when you meet? How much time needs to be spent on each of the segments of the teaching sessions? What resources will be needed? How will the space be arranged? What are the back-up plans in case of cancellations due to illnesses of teachers or students? How will absentees be contacted? Will specific witnessing features be carried out or will you let witnessing come as a natural outcome of ministry relationships as they are established? This is certainly not a comprehensive list of questions, but it will give you an idea of where to begin. Add other questions that reflect the particulars of your setting.

Engaging the Servant Helpers

Now that you have the program design on paper, the next step is to make a list of all the volunteers you will need to initiate the program. The hypothetical program format for teaching international women requires one person who will serve as coordinator of the program. This person will serve as a hostess and record keeper and will take care of emergencies. Four people will be needed to serve as teachers. Two people will supervise the nursery. Another two people will be responsible for setting up the dining room for lunch and preparing beverages. One person will need to see that enough English-speaking women come to lunch so that the international women can practice what they are learning in conversational English classes. Volunteers and students will bring their own lunches so there will be no need for people to prepare food.

Now is the time to secure definite commitments from the servant helpers. In the helping field these commitments are called *covenants* or *contracts*. Before you go further in the ministry, each volunteer should make a definitive commitment to work in the program. Everyone needs to have a job description and know how long the project will last. The more specific the commitment, the more likely it is that volunteers will carry it out.

Plan an orientation time for the volunteers. Make sure all their questions and concerns are addressed. Help them be as prepared as possible. Ask the volunteers to review the program format and make any suggestions they feel will improve the program. At this time make certain that everyone can be present and prepared on the date you will first meet with the international women. This is extremely important because the first meeting will set the tone for all that follows.

If the servant helpers need training to do their tasks well, now is the time to find out what these training needs are and assist the people in making arrangements to get the training. For example, the people who are going to keep the nursery might want to work in the church nursery for several Sundays to get some ideas about activities or discipline for small children. The teachers may need training from literacy specialists in the state convention or may want to find a local college or university offering certification courses for ESL instructors. Whatever the training needs are, now is the time to address them. Remember that people tend to enjoy doing what they know how to do well. The converse is also true.

The ministry's sponsoring group should hold a commissioning service for these servant helpers before they begin the actual ministry. Make this a special time and emphasize the seriousness of the volunteers' promises to help. To a large extent, the future effectiveness of the program will depend on these servant helpers.

It is important to remember that these servant helpers or volunteers will need prayer support as they carry out their work. They will also need to meet together to discuss solutions to problems that arise and to share successes and accomplishments. Adapt and refine the formatting based on what is learned in program implementation. Such meeting times should be put on the calendar as a part of the engagement process. Recall earlier mention of the fact that getting involved in ministries helps Christians grow into mature disciples. These group meetings will be times for them to identify and affirm this growth in each other.

When the process of engaging servant leaders is completed, you should have competent people who have agreed to serve in each of the roles needed to implement the program. These servant leaders should understand that this agreement is a sacred covenant of ministry between them, their church, and God.

Engaging the Clients

A key element of the program design is the plan to engage the people who will receive the services. Sometimes ministries are started with the false assumption that if the service is made available, people will automatically know about it and access it. This has proven in most cases to be false. At this point, based on your program format and the number of volunteers you have, a decision needs to be made as to the number of people you can really help. You will not be able to help all the people all the time.

It may be difficult to limit the size of your program, but remember it is far better to select a small group and really help them. With too many people no one gets the attention she or he needs in order to insure that program goals are reached. Being successful with a small group will establish a good reputation for the program. You can always repeat the program for another group if it is needed.

Review the information in the needs assessment as it relates to the illustration of English classes for international women. Does the person or group who identified this need know how to contact these women? Is there some place where a list of names and addresses is available? Is there someone at the automotive plant who could be a contact person for you? Would a story in a local newspaper about the proposed ministry reach any of these people? Are there places for brochures to be left such as doctors' offices, beauty shops, or grocery stores? What about putting notices in neighborhood church bulletins? Think of as many ways as possible to advertise the availability of the new ministry. In all the publicity, be as informative as possible. Always include a telephone number people can call for more information.

Meet with the officials of the manufacturing company and offer the ESL program to the wives in the employee families. See if the company officials will allow you to have a reception for the women and their spouses during a break time at the plant. If you can get to know one or two people who are interested, they will involve their friends.

When you think you have some potential clients, plan an orientation meeting for about twice the number of people you will be able to help in your program. You will need to invite more than you can enroll because some will not come and some will not be interested when they find out the details. You will need a list of alternates in case some have to leave the program because of illnesses or company transfers.

This orientation time will give you a chance to begin building relationships. Make sure in each of these meetings that you have people who can translate as well as help you become more culturally sensitive in your communications and actions.

The information you make available to the people who come to the orientation time should be clear and specific. For example, do not just give an address for the meeting place. Tell the women which door to enter from which street. Tell them there will be someone stationed at the door to take them to their classroom. Tell them where they can park their cars. All policies and procedures your group has established should be shared. Your policy on confidentiality is an example of a policy which should be discussed with them. They will also be interested in your child-care practices. Other issues can be added to this list as you think of them.

The more information you give them, the less anxiety they will have about coming. If there is a book to buy, tell them specifically how much it will cost and where they can get it. If child care will be available, show them where their children will stay and who will take care of them. Be precise about when you will begin and end each session. Give them a telephone number where their families can reach them in times of emergencies. If they will be using public transportation, help them understand which buses to take and where to get off. A good rule of thumb is to tell these women everything you would want to know if you were one of them.

Before the orientation meeting adjourns, make sure you have asked each person present to decide if she wants to participate in the English as a second language classes. If some need more time, get permission to call them later in the week to see if they have more questions.

The keys to engaging clients are to have plans which will identify them, communicate to them the nature of the services to be offered, encourage the formation of relationships between them and the servant helpers, and create environments where they will feel safe while being helped.

In addition, all of this must be done with special care to convey to them that they are people of ultimate worth who will be treated with dignity and respect.

Please keep in mind that as soon as possible it is important to invite some of the international women to become servant helpers as well. After the program gets started, the international women can assist with child care or help with lunch preparation. Later when they become competent in English as a second language, they should be invited and trained to become teachers themselves. One of the goals for ministry should always be to turn clients into helpers. In this way ministries can be multiplied and people can be empowered.

Implementing the Program Design

By this time in the process, the design decisions should be made. However, if some things such as approvals have not been put in place, now is the time to follow up on these issues.

The implementation of the ministry is simply doing what you had planned to do or *working the plan*. During the initial phase of implementation, focuses should include building relationships with the international women, providing the supports they will need to risk participating in the program, and encouraging the servant helpers. After the first few meetings, people will settle into a routine and the program will become enjoyable for all involved.

Every program needs to be refined in the process of implementation. For example, suppose you discover that the women are having a hard time getting their children off to school and getting to ESL classes by 9:30 A.M. This conflict might call for a readjustment in the starting time. Perhaps the teachers decided that one more learner can be added to each of the groups. In this case, the coordinator will need to call the first alternates to see if they would like to start attending classes. You will likely discover other things that will necessitate fine tuning. Do not hesitate to make these adjustments and adaptations.

Evaluation

Evaluation is important in determining the accountability and effectiveness of a ministry and is especially compelling for Christians who carry out their ministries in Jesus' name. People who start programs are accountable for the people, finances, and other resources they utilize. Good stewardship demands this. They are also accountable to uphold standards and regulations that may apply to their ministry.

For example, health and safety rules and regulations apply equally to church-sponsored ministries and to those operated in the public sector. Day-care centers sponsored by the church must meet health and safety standards and be licensed by the state to operate. Congregate meal sites must adhere to health standards, as well.

The separation of church and state statutes exempt church ministries from some rules and regulations regarding minimum standards of service which are applied to public helping programs that receive state or federal funds. Laws against discrimination are examples of such exemptions. While these exemptions do exist, church ministries should always strive to exceed the minimum state standards. Because we are implementing these ministries in Jesus' name, what we do and the care with which we do it reflects on our church, our faith, and our Lord. Using the separation of church and state doctrines and laws as justification for lowering the standards of health, safety, nondiscrimination, and civil rights in our church ministries is an abuse of these statutes.

To measure program effectiveness, the question to ask is, "Were the goals of the program realized?" In the illustration of English classes for international women, did the international women learn English as a second language well enough to begin to participate in social networks and carry out their roles of mother, neighbor, and citizen? Kettner says, "If the program planning and design resulted in nothing of value for the people involved and the community as a whole, then it has been a waste of time."[14]

In order to answer accountability and effectiveness questions, data must be gathered and analyzed based on the measurable objectives determined earlier by the leadership group. Start by taking each of the measures of success in the objectives. For each measure, a method to gather the data must be developed. The success of ten women learning to read the daily newspaper could be measured in several ways. If the teacher is using daily newspapers in the classroom, then he or she can simply keep a list of those who have learned to read it with an acceptable level of comprehension. Another way would be to have a test at the end of the program which required that they read several articles and, in their own words, tell what they mean.

Make out a one-page evaluation form to gather data reflecting how well you cared for the in-kind space and have representatives of the owners of the in-kind space complete the form once a quarter. Appropriate questions to include on this evaluation form are: Were items put back in the order they were found? Was the space cleaned after use? Was wear and tear of equipment within the expected range? Were lights turned off after use? Were doors locked? Have the people who complete this form rank your performance as poor = 1, satisfactory = 2, or excellent = 3. At the conclusion of the program, average the scores on the quarterly reports. You will know whether or not you responsibly handled the in-kind resources made available to you.

The results of these kinds of evaluations will be critical when it comes time to decide whether or not the program should be replicated for another cycle. Even if you repeat the program, the information gathered through the evaluation will assist you in making improvements in this second series.

Summary

A program design in its simplest form outlines the arrangements and actions needed to meet the goals of the program. Prior to designing the program, a leadership group must be put in place; program configurations decided upon; change objectives selected; approvals and sponsorships secured; risks assessed and addressed; money management practices put in place; and reporting and record keeping procedures determined. Once all these tasks are accomplished, a format for how the program will be constructed should be put on paper. After this is done, the servant helpers and the clients should be engaged. The program should then be implemented for the agreed upon length of time. During the implementation and after the completion of the program, evaluations should be carried out to determine the effectiveness and efficiency of the program.

When all the steps in Chapters 4 and 5 are carried out, an entire program cycle is completed. Now is the time to decide whether or not to repeat the cycle. If programs are done well and meet a real need, the answer is usually yes.

Learning Activities

1. What is meant by a *match* when considering needs and resources? What matches do you anticipate finding between the resources of your group or church and the needs of your community?

2. What are your church's procedures for sponsoring new ministries? What responsibilities are assigned to the missions committee in your church? Who will comprise the steering committee if a new ministry is started?

3. Think about risk management. What is it and what issues or risks would a group face if they decided to start a new ministry sponsored by your church?

4. Pick out a hypothetical program and think your way through a possible format for this program. Practice revising the format until you arrive at something you think will work.

5. Decide on a strategy for engaging servant helpers. Review the material on spiritual gifts. How would you approach a person to recruit her as a servant helper? What really motivates people? What is the role of prayer in this matter?

6. Visit the library and read a book on recruiting, training, and supervising volunteers. What part of this material did you find helpful?

7. Identify barriers which might keep people from accessing community resources. How will you enable people to overcome these barriers? What might be done in a new ministry program to prevent these barriers from arising?

8. Decide on a new ministry program. Write out goals and objectives for this program. Do your objectives make clear the way in which the program will be evaluated? What evaluation instruments will you need to construct? What is meant by efficiency and effectiveness in program evaluation?

7

Helping: Acts of
Faith and Risks

The hope which underlies this entire book is that
Christians who read it will be challenged and prepared to start new ministries outside the walls of their
churches. The ministering and witnessing model of Jesus
as recorded in the Gospel of Luke is a foundation upon
which all our ministry and witness efforts must be built.

Christian helping is an act of faith. I learned a long
time ago that I will likely never know the outcomes of the
ministry and witness efforts that I make. I am called to be
responsible for being true to my time in history. However,
I must always remember that in God's scheme of things,
my time is just a sliver of eternity. I am called to invest
today and then let God do with the investment what God
is capable of doing. In a way, all our ministry efforts are
gifts to God and we have faith they will be used for God's
purposes.

This point is beautifully illustrated in the actions of
Jeremiah. You recall that Jeremiah was under arrest
because he had interpreted King Jedekiah's dream to
mean that Jedekiah was going to lose and the King of
Babylon was going to win. King Jedekiah did not like this
news, so he placed Jeremiah under the supervision of the
palace guard. Jeremiah knew that the exile was coming.

Hanamel, a cousin of Jeremiah, came and asked
Jeremiah to buy the home place because it was his
responsibility to hold the land for the family. Hanamel
probably did not want to go into exile without some
financial resources. Why would Jeremiah buy this field
that Hanamel wanted to sell? Anyway you look at it, it
appeared to be a foolish investment. Jeremiah would
never live long enough to use the land or benefit from it.
But, as an act of faith, Jeremiah bought the field. He said

that he did it because the word of the Lord said to do it. Most scholars estimate that it was around 400 years before land was bought and sold again in that part of the world. But for Jeremiah, it was a matter of following God's instructions. He would never know the outcome but he bought the field. Read the entire story in Jeremiah 32.

Ministry and witness efforts are like buying a field. You invest now because it is what God wants you to do. You may never live to see the outcomes. You do what you do out of faith that God will use it to work out God's will. If you need to realize a positive outcome of your ministry and witness efforts in order to keep up your momentum, you will soon get discouraged. If you give your ministry and witness efforts to God as a gift, and trust God to use them, you can go on and on without getting discouraged. Decide now that you do not have to know how it all will come out.

Acts of Preparation and Risk

Not only are ministry and witness efforts acts of faith, they are acts of preparation and risk. Matthew 25 begins with two parables. The first of these is a parable of preparation involving wise and foolish young maidens. The teaching of the parable is that we are to always be prepared for the end time. I like this parable. It is in my nature to be prepared because being prepared reduces the possibility of risk.

However, the second parable is a parable of risk. It calls for us to overcome our fears and invest in an uncertain market so that when the property owner returns, we can return to him not only his initial investment, but also interest earnings. This parable teaches us that we are to risk and resist having our fears and uncertainties keep us from doing what is right and helpful.

Starting a new ministry involves a mixture of preparation and risk. While we are to be as prepared as we can be, there is a point at which we have to risk ourselves and invest in uncertainties. These are uncertainties over which we have no control. We have to relinquish control over our efforts and give them wings to fly to places we cannot know. This is the risk.

No Last Words

There is no ending to this book. Ministry and witness are always beginning. The endings are God's to fashion. My prayer for you is that you will start and stay on the journey. If you do, somewhere out there, God will take your gifts of effort and bless and multiply them. Jesus promises that if we love God with all that is in us and love our neighbors as we love ourselves, we shall live!

ENDNOTES

[1] Henri J. M. Nouwen, *The Wounded Healer: Ministry in Contemporary Society* (New York: Doubleday & Co., 1972).

[2] Roberta Hestenes, "The Congregation as a Caring Community" (paper presented at the Church as a Caring Community conference, Louisville, Ken., Sept. 1990).

[3] William L. Hendricks, "A Theological Basis for Christian Social Ministries," *Review and Expositor* (Southern Baptist Theological Seminary, Louisville, Ken.) 85, no. 2 (spring 1988): 221.

[4] Culbert G. Rutenberg, *The Reconciling Gospel* (Nashville: Broadman Press, 1960), 59.

[5] Alan Keith-Lucas, *Giving and Taking Help* (Chapel Hill: The University of North Carolina Press, 1972), 47–65.

[6] Page Kelly, *Layman's Bible Book Commentary*, vol. 14 (Nashville: Broadman Press, 1984), 43–44.

[7] "Manual of Operations: Baptist Centers and Pastor/Center Ministries," ed. C. Anne Davis and Patricia L. Bailey (Atlanta: Home Mission Board, SBC, Christian Social Ministries Center, 1987), 50.

[8] Clifford M. Johnson et al., *Child Poverty In America* (Washington, DC: National Children's Defense Fund, 1991), 13.

[9] Mark Robert Rank, *Living on the Edge: The Realities of Welfare in America* (New York: Columbia University Press, 1994), 234.

[10] Larry W. Bennett, "Substance Abuse and the Domestic Assault of Women," *Social Work* 40, no. 6 (November 1995): 760.

[11] Arnold Barnes and Paul Ephross, "The Impact of Hate Violence on Victims: Emotional and Behavioral Responses to Attacks," *Social Work* 39, no. 3 (May 1994): 250.

[12] Edwin J. Thomas, *Designing Interventions for the Helping Profession* (Beverly Hills: SAGE Publications, 1994), 30–31.

[13] Peter M. Kettner, Robert M. Moroney, and Lawrence L. Martin, *Designing and Managing Programs: An Effectiveness-Based Approach* (Newbury Park: SAGE Publications, 1990), 88.

[14] Ibid., 9.